C000262283

JOHN BAILEY'S FISHING GUIDES

IMPROVE YOUR LURE FISHING

JOHN BAILEY'S FISHING GUIDES

IMPROVE YOUR LURE FISHING

LEARN THE UNDERWATER SECRETS OF FISH AND THEIR HABITATS

First published in 2003 by
New Holland Publishers (UK) Ltd

London • Cape Town • Sydney • Auckland

www.newhollandpublishers.com

10 9 8 7 6 5 4 3 2 1

Garfield House, 86–88 Edgware Road, London W2 2EA

80 McKenzie Street, Cape Town 8001, South Africa

14 Aquatic Drive, Frenchs Forest, NSW 2086, Australia

218 Lake Road, Northcote, Auckland, New Zealand

Copyright © 2003 New Holland Publishers (UK) Ltd

All rights reserved. No part of this publication may be reproduced, stored in a retrieval system or transmitted, in any form or by any means, electronic, mechanical, photocopying or otherwise, without the prior written permission of the publishers and copyright holders.

ISBN 1 84330 353 1

Edited and designed by Design Revolution Limited,
Queen's Park Villa, 30 West Drive, Brighton BN2 2GE
Project Editor: Ian Whitelaw
Designer: Lindsey Johns
Editor: Julie Whitaker
Illustrations by Rob Olsen

Index by Indexing Specialists,
202 Church Road, Hove BN3 2DJ

Publishing Manager: Jo Hemmings
Senior Editor: Kate Michell
Assistant Editor: Anne Konopelski
Production Controller: Lucy Hulme

Reproduction by Pica Digital (Pte) Ltd, Singapore
Printed and bound in Singapore by Craft Print
(Pte) Ltd

Contents

INTRODUCTION

I was nine years old when I joined Compstall Angling Club just outside Stockport in the north of England. The water the club possessed was a former mill dam with crystal-clear water and towering walls from which you could see every leaf of weed and grain of sand. It was there that I first learnt the importance of being able to watch your predators at play and at work. In this case, the species were perch and though many of them were small, the reservoir held some monsters. And it was only by watching and planning that you could engineer their downfall. It was this experience at such a tender age that made me want to keep fish in tanks and which has certainly led me to believe that the understanding of fish is the most important step in catching them.

▲ **Keeping It Simple** It's not always necessary to kit yourself out with full scuba gear to study fish in their natural habitat. If the weather is warm and bright, as it was in Spain where the air temperature topped 40°C, shorts, T-shirt and goggles will do the job. Always beware of getting out of your depth or finding yourself in deceptively quick currents – and protect the back of your neck from the sun.

So, five years or so ago, I began diving and photographing what I saw under the surface. In large part, therefore, this book is an amalgam of the experiences I've built up over forty years of watching fish from both above and below the surface and through a pane of glass. I like to think that every image tells a story and increases our understanding.

There are many things, of course, that photographs cannot get across – the effect of sound being one of these things. When you dive, you realize just how great a conductor of sound water is and the extraordinary impact of heavy footfalls on a gravel bank or even loud voices. Predators, in my experience, are not always as anxious about disturbance as prey fish can be, but it is still foolish to sabotage your chances in any way, shape or form. So my advice is to tread carefully, to wade cautiously and to keep your voice down. Think carefully, also, about the splash that your lure makes: at times this can be an inducement to an attack, but on other occasions it can make a fish wary. If you suspect the latter then try to think of quieter ways of introducing your lure into the water. If you're in a river, for example, then you can drift the lure down with the current rather than casting it before retrieval. If you're in a boat, think about cutting that engine before getting to your hot spot or, better still, investing in an electric motor. If you're rowing, then do so catching as few crabs as you possibly can!

▲ **TESTING** To get a really accurate idea of how your plugs behave in every situation, try to watch them operating in various depths of water.

THE WORLD OF WATER

Actually going under the surface and spending time in the water itself will show you that it is far from a one-dimensional element. Water is a whole world in itself and offers quite unexpected underwater geography. It's a mass of twisting currents, unexpected drop-offs and noticeable changes in water temperature. If you're going to fish lures adequately then it really does pay off to think very carefully about the water that is in front of you. And don't regard a river as simply an aquatic escalator moving remorselessly towards the sea: look carefully at boulders, drop-offs, fallen trees, bends, weirs, sluices and all the other things that interrupt and deflect its progress. Water is an alien element but that doesn't mean that it is unknowable: spend time just watching water and, as you become more confident, catches will rocket.

YOUR THINKING FISH

Always remember that the predatory fish that you're pursuing do learn. They may prove hard to catch for all sorts of reasons, and simple wariness is often a part of this. Lure fishing can, or should be, very touchy-feely: braid lines, for example, make for an intimate understanding of what your lure is doing. For instance, you can often feel a lure working through shoals of prey fish or even bouncing off the backs of predators. If you're getting the signals that there are fish down there but not taking, then stop and reconsider your approach. Don't narrow your options or become blinkered. Regard every trip out with your lure box as a challenge and as a completely new chapter to be written.

I've talked about rubber baits in the book, primarily for predators, but do remember that virtually every fish that swims is willing to have a crack at them. Certainly, rubber worms and the like can be used for carp, bream and even rudd. Keep an open mind – that's what lure fishing is all about.

▼ **A True Friend** I owe a debt of gratitude to Johnny Jensen, Danish photographer, writer, angler, diver and, above all, my travelling partner, inspiration and great, great friend.

TREAT WITH CARE

Pike, and other predators come to that, might look big and mean and toothy but they are vulnerable. Their organs are delicate, their gills are vulnerable and they suffer from stress. In fact, as far as pike are concerned, it's we humans who represent their major threat in life. Consequently, don't go fishing for predators until you are confident that you can unhook and return them in a responsible, risk-free way. Always make sure that you have the right tools for the job, such as pliers, forceps and unhooking mats. Go with experienced friends until you are confident you can lure alone! Here are just a few tips, in no particular order:

- Lure fishing is a fast-changing world and new lures, tackle and techniques appear all the time. Buy the magazines, search the web and send out orders for catalogues. To stay in touch with developments in the UK you can join the Lure Anglers' Society, and there are similar groups in Europe and North America.

▲ **Exceptions to the Rule** This particular stickleback stayed with a shoal of predatory chub for several days; apparently accepted, he survived unharmed.

- Look after your lures because they are expensive. Store them in the dry. Check hooks, split rings and swivels constantly for rust or weakening.
- Always take two of each of your lure models with you. There's nothing worse than finding THE lure of the day only to lose it!

FOR THE TECHNICAL

I won't go into the intricacies of diving equipment here: a standard dry suit and all the equipment that goes with it will be needed. Sometimes extra-heavy weights are vital to pin you down to the bottom. Less important are flippers: I've done very little swimming over the last three or four years – more time is spent just sitting waiting on the bottom of the river-bed!

I have used Nikon F90Xs exclusively with a range of Nikon lenses. The most useful have been 24mm and 28mm. I have generally used the Nikon speed light SB-28 when extra light has been needed. For a lot of the work I have made use of a Subal metal unit; this is very solid and trustworthy. For lighter, more mobile work, I have used a Ewa-marine plastic bag; this may sound a bit flimsy, but it has only let me down once! Believe me, a flood is what every underwater photographer fears more than anything. Films have been uniformly Fuji. Provia 100 has been preferred, but at times of low light I've employed 200 ASA or 400 ASA speeds.

I hope that some of my underwater observations will throw light on the challenges that we, as anglers, meet on the bank side. Good luck.

John Bailey, Salthouse, Norfolk

PREDATOR BEHAVIOUR

In fresh water, at least, there are basic differences between predators – such as pike, perch and zander – and grazers – such as carp, rudd or bream. The grazers tend to keep on the move, looking for food throughout most of the day, and even when not feeding, they tend to be alert and on their guard. The pattern of their lives is one of feeding and survival, and there's not a great deal of opportunity left for chilling out!

The predator, on the other hand, has a very different lifestyle. Firstly, its meals tend to be large and satisfying, and a single gulp may provide sustenance for hours, if not days or even weeks, so hunting time is not as extended as it is with the grazers. Secondly, the predator's food – almost always meat – generally takes longer to digest, especially in cold weather, so the digestive system tells the predator to sit back and take it easy for appreciable periods. And thirdly, whilst the predator is not without its enemies, notably men and otters, it is high up the aquatic food chain and has comparatively little to worry about – unlike the half-pound rudd that is forever looking over its shoulder in trepidation.

◀ **An Early Frost** A sudden cold snap in early winter can have a decisive effect on all predators. The water temperature can drop several degrees overnight and all fish life slows down. If you can get a lure through the ice, work it deep and slow, knocking bottom if possible.

The Alarm Clock Ticks

Predators have the ability to lie on the bottom, or even drift in currents, virtually comatose, almost totally shut down from the world around them. It's not only the obvious species, such as pike, that behave like this: I have some knowledge of ferox trout, the big predatory browns of the glacial lochs, and they do very little between bouts of feeding apart from drifting in the deep, dark water barely rippling a fin. Eels are another example; these might hunt very actively, which is usually when they're hungry, but for long periods they simply lie under rocks, down submerged drainpipes or anywhere that shields them from the light of day.

When predators behave like this, which is usually when the weather is cold and the digestive system takes longer to work, there's very little that the angler can do. Very little will switch a comatose predator into feeding mode. It's most often a question of patience, or of choosing days when conditions look most favourable.

▶ **Dead to the World** This pike is barely moving at all. It's been in exactly the same place for two days and shows no sign of breaking out of its torpor. Pike like this just don't respond to anything. If you're in a canoe, for example, you can lift one virtually out of the water with your paddle before it will waddle off, back down to the bottom. If you're diving, you can virtually poke them on the nose without raising a response.

▶ **An Unpromising Scene** These are the conditions that the angler really doesn't like to see – cold, clear days with freezing nights and a build-up of ice. The big question is 'do all predators turn off at the same time in any given water?' To some degree, they do, but there's always hope: smaller predators feed more often, as their prey is smaller and they must hunt more regularly.

◀ **Days of Dark and Light** Of course, if a period of cold weather goes on for a long time then predators become accustomed to it and they will need to feed eventually, no matter how bad the conditions. All the grazers know this, and will therefore look for areas to hole up in that offer the greatest chance of shelter and protection. Even big carp will be found under trailing branches or snuggled among the remains of lily beds or clumps of weed. During long periods of cold weather, the underwater world slows down to a snail's pace, waiting to be kick-started into life by a rise in water temperatures.

▲ **Slumbering Perch** A cold snap in the late autumn can hit the perch hard, and they won't move for days. Notice how they take up shelter in branches and fallen leaves, where it is difficult to get a bait to them. At times like this, jigging can succeed if you can find debris close in to the bank that you can work from your rod tip. Alternatively, try a worm held just clear of the snags by a float.

The Wake-up Call

Finally, something begins to happen. Little by little, the predators start to come alive. As I've said, it could just be that bad conditions have gone on and on, and they're naturally feeling hungry. Alternatively, something in the water conditions begins to stimulate them. Perhaps the ice is breaking up. Perhaps water temperatures are rising subtly. Perhaps heavy rain has begun to tinge the water and increase oxygen levels. There won't be an immediate click over from one form of behaviour to another, but you will see all the signs of life beginning to re-emerge; the grazers certainly feel it. There's a buzz about the water, and the shoals of prey fish are moving in a much more animated fashion; as far as they're concerned, it will soon be business as usual.

▲ **Becoming Alert** Now the pike is much more aware of the world around it, and we can easily make out the signs that the grazers recognize. The pike has shaken off the weed and fallen leaves that had built up around and over it. It has altered its body position and is now hanging a few inches off the bottom. Its fins are beginning to work, especially the pectorals and pelvic fins as it holds position. Its tail fin beats out a slow, menacing rhythm. The eye appears to have more life in it, and certainly begins to move around its socket. You can almost see the saliva beginning to form on those bony jaws!

◀ **Diving Hunter** It's not only the pike that's waking to the world around it. This grebe is making the most of a good feeding opportunity with a succulent roach. The small grazers, well aware of the threat from above, are harried into constant movement, stirring the predator into ever more aggressive behaviour. The grebe, itself, also stimulates the predator as it splashes and dives and generally titillates the appetite!

◀ **Catching the Light** The once common and beloved Ratty of *The Wind in the Willows* fame faces the twin menaces of reed-bed destruction and the arrival of the mink, and those voles that remain are liable to end up inside a pike. Notice how the light strikes the vole's fur and how the oxygen bubbles glitter and rise to the surface. More and more alarm bells are ringing, and the pace of the prowl is beginning to hot up.

◀ **Extensive Reed Beds** There could well be large pike in among the reeds, and for the angler early spring is a key time as pike start to wake up and think of moving out on the prowl. In the past, in the Norfolk Broads, some old pike experts used to actually drive their boats into the reeds at this time, to flush the pike out into open water, anger them and possibly spark them into a feeding frenzy.

On the Prowl

The predator is now on the prowl, its body programmed, focusing on the food. It doesn't matter where you are, you will see that the grazers are becoming ever more nervous. On a Scottish loch, for example, char shoals become more flighty, constantly flitting here and there, fearful of the lunge of a ferox trout into their midst. Minnows in a clear river will be instantly aware of a group of hungry perch closing in on them, and they'll dive for the nearest cover. And, of course, down there it's a fish-eat-fish world! The small pike is afraid of the bigger pike. The small perch is afraid of the big perch and of pike of any size. All the small fish are afraid of the eels, which, in their turn, are afraid of the pike. Only a pike of double figures can really feel safe – or can it? It is not unusual to see fresh scars on the flanks of even a seventeen-pounder!

▸ **Through the Lilies** Now our pike is very much on the prowl, with a roving eye to the main chance. Everything about it suggests menace. It moves slowly, cautiously, speeding up whenever it senses life nearby. All its fins are moving, and tremors travel down its body as its muscles twitch; its eyes move and its mouth opens and closes with increasing frequency.

▸ **Water-birds** Nothing is safe – not the wandering water vole, nor an ill-advised coot. Pike do eat water-birds, and more frequently than is generally supposed. But, of course, it all depends on size. This particular pike is attracted by the commotion the coot makes, and also by the light glinting off its plumage. It considers a strike, but the coot, it realizes, is simply too big. Now, if there were a duckling scuttling about...

◀ **The Predator** The perch shoal has also decided to move and to begin feeding. Fish of half a pound or so will be looking for all manner of prey – minnows and fingerlings, but also nymphs, caddis, shrimp and beetles. Perch this size have to work harder now than when they're larger and can snap up a couple of dace, which is one reason small perch are always easier to catch than large ones.

◀ **And the Prey** While our small perch are hunting for their food, they remain very aware that they could become prey themselves. An eight-ounce perch is certainly not too large to be harried by its three-pound grandmother, and pike, zander, herons, otters and very big eels are also potential dangers. Smaller perch, then, seem torn between hunting for food and sheltering from the hunters. It's a difficult life.

◀ **Visual Signal** I'm convinced that light sparks predators into decisive feeding action. Sounds and vibrations transmitted through the water also play an extremely important part, as does smell, especially in murky water. In clear water, however, above all, I put my money on the light effect. Sunlight dancing on the silvery scales of fish such as these chub is something no big predator can resist.

The Hunt in Earnest

We tend to think of pike as the archetypal hunting predator, but not all fish-eaters attack in the same way. In fact, many of them aren't ideally suited to their job at all! For example, ferox trout have a comparatively small mouth and are not much faster than a normal small brown trout. They need huge shoals of prey fish to dive into if they are to stand much chance of success – hence their entire reliance on char shoals. Nor do perch have an amazing turn of speed or mouths capable of grabbing, holding and ripping like a pike's. As a result, perch are happier hunting in shoals, as this gives them a better chance of manoeuvring prey fish into vulnerable, defenceless positions. The world of the predator is a diverse one: there's no simple, single form of attack, and even a pike will use a variety of different tactics and techniques.

▶ **The Attack Angle** Doing exactly what an angler wants to see and a rudd does not, the pike that angles itself upwards in this way has only one thing on its mind – a spurt, an attack and a kill. It's fascinating that roach, rudd and bream will swim over a resting pike on the lake bed as though it's not there, certain that no attack is imminent, but when a pike looks like this, they can tell it's out to take their lives.

▶ **Defensive Strategy** This is a rudd shoal in pre-flight formation, acutely aware of what's happening. Firstly, they rise higher in the water, trying to get out of harm's way. One member of the group looks into the water behind the others. This is typical: the whole 360° have to be covered. Once that pike is physically spotted, the shoal will take evasive action, either wheeling away as a group or scattering in different directions.

◀ **A Vulnerable Roach** Your pike is on the prowl now, feeling hungry, mounting attacks. Here, amongst a shoal of roach, filtered sunlight catches the flank of one individual – providing an instant trigger and a glowing target for the pike. A fish dappled by shade is a much more indistinct target and is unlikely to provoke an attack. Should an attack occur, it also stands more chance of escape.

◀ **Defenceless** Commonly, an angler will lose his fish to a pike or other predator as he brings it to the net. Watching this barbel being drawn into the folds, you can see why. The fish presents a perfectly illuminated target and is also, obviously, quite defenceless. Pike and other big predators are used to picking off dead and dying fish, and something as defenceless as a defeated fish coming to the net is more than they can resist.

◀ **Ready for Flight** This shoal of dace is behaving exactly as I would expect of a group of nervous fish. They are fanning out, pointing in all directions rather than simply against the current. They are not feeding either – a sure sign that they sense menace. This shoal will rely on the starburst effect to confuse and baffle a predator. So, should a pike attack, they'll scatter, regrouping once danger has passed.

DEAD BAITING

Although dead baiting is not as satisfying as lure fishing, it does give an option when conditions are hard – and it needn't always be a static or tedious method. You can, for example, use a dead bait twitched sink-and-draw fashion in very much the same way as a rubber jig or even a plug. All serious anglers have a few dead baits stored away in a freezer. Freeze baits individually wrapped in cling film. Ensure that they're stored flat – kinked dead baits are difficult to cast any distance, awkward to hook and, being so unnatural, aren't very attractive to a predator. Popular dead baits include sea fish such as mackerel, herrings and sprats. Natural freshwater dead baits are also excellent, so store any that you find freshly dead in the margins. Eel sections are also good. Variety is the spice of life when it comes to dead baiting, and there's always room for exotics such as the horse mackerel – a round, oily fish that gives off a good, strong smell.

▲ **Efficiently Struck** Always hit a run at the first indication of a bite. Delay and there's a chance that the dead bait will be snaffled and taken into the throat where unhooking becomes a perilous business.

Weather Conditions

The successful predator angler is the one who can make all manner of successful calculations and come up with the correct answers. You've got to think about the water, its clarity, features, structures, fish numbers, target species, methods, lure types, shapes, colours, actions and, last but certainly not least, weather conditions. As a very rough rule, if your water has severely coloured up due to very heavy rains or high winds, then it could be that dead bait will have a slight advantage over lure fishing. If a predator has to hunt by sight alone, this makes lure fishing in very cloudy water an extremely difficult task. Dead baits work well when visibility is low because, of course, they emit a good, strong scent. Lure fishing is huge fun, but don't become blinkered and refuse to use other methods if the weather conditions scream out for them.

▲ **Flat Calm** There can be times when the water is like a millpond and predators, pike especially, can become very reluctant to move. Obviously, if there's no wind interference, the sound of oars, an engine, casting and even anglers talking is greatly enhanced. As a diver I have experienced this for myself: as you lie in a lake on a calm day, you will hear all sorts of muffled sounds – every sound above and below the surface is hugely exaggerated. For this reason, if you're going after a big, suspicious fish, it sometimes pays simply to cast out a dead bait and wait for the pike to make a move.

▸ **Cold Weather** As autumn turns to winter, you'll find that pike, for example, don't want to expend unnecessary energy hunting a fast-moving bait. It's these first few days or weeks of falling temperatures when a dead bait stands a good chance of being taken. Once predators have acclimatized to the cold weather, slow-moving lures are once again accepted.

▸ **A Freeze Up** When the temperatures have really plummeted and the water is largely covered by ice, the lure angler certainly has a hard task. Lure fishing is a roving, mobile way of fishing, and if most of the water is absolutely inaccessible, this method obviously becomes extremely difficult. However, you still want to go fishing, so the best bet in these conditions is a dead bait under a float cast into a hole in the ice. Do make sure, however, that the ice is not too thick to stop you landing a hooked fish.

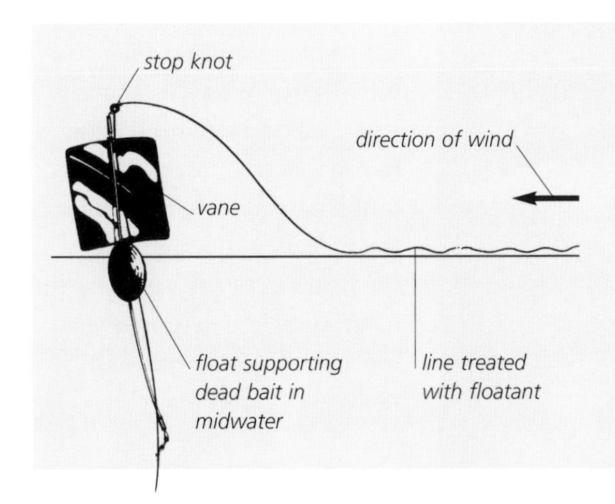

The Drift Float

This rig works particularly well for searching out large waters when there's a decent breeze blowing. The vane catches the wind and will trot before it, providing the line is well-greased, covering huge areas of the water. It is quite possible to drift the float over 150 yards or more, but it's wise to have binoculars with you at these distances so that you can see a take. Once the float disappears, wind down tight and strike immediately to avoid deep hooking.

Presentation Considerations

A pike has plenty of time to examine a dead bait, as it is either static or very slow moving. Anything suspicious will be ignored. The simplest rig to use is the legered dead bait. I use a float for indication, as this is absolutely immediate and creates little disturbance. Dead bait generally provides enough weight for long casts. Putting extra lead on the line simply pulls it into bottom weed. If weed is a problem, you can 'pop up' a dead bait by inserting buoyant material, such as a balsa wood stick, polystyrene or foam, into the stomach cavity or mouth. Make baits partially buoyant so they will sink very slowly and come to rest at the top of any weed. A totally buoyant bait held a few inches off the bottom by lead weights can be good, but only for limited periods as pike soon get wise to this approach.

◀ **Matching the Hatch** I don't rate trout very highly as dead baits, but they do seem to work in waters where pike are used to feeding on them. I believe that the lack of smell is a big disadvantage, so it's a good idea to inject them with an added dose of fish oils. Do take great care, though, when using a syringe – injecting an air bubble into your own bloodstream will prove fatal – so never dream of injecting a dead bait in a boat if there's a swell on.

◀ **Landing Your Fish** A well beaten dead-bait caught pike comes to the bank. Look how the trebles are flying free. This is indicative of a well-timed strike, but if a net is used now, a real tangle is almost guaranteed, probably wounding the pike in the process. Far better to lift the pike out of the water by hand. Until you become skilled, use a stout leather glove to save your fingers.

▸ Improvisation Techniques It's not often that you see a small, dead grayling used as a bait. This shot was taken in Mongolia, where they are the general prey fish for the predatory taiman. Once again, it's good to match the hatch. On this particular day we ran out of leads, but we simply put some bank-side stones into a small polythene bag and tied it above the trace. There is always a solution to any fishing problem.

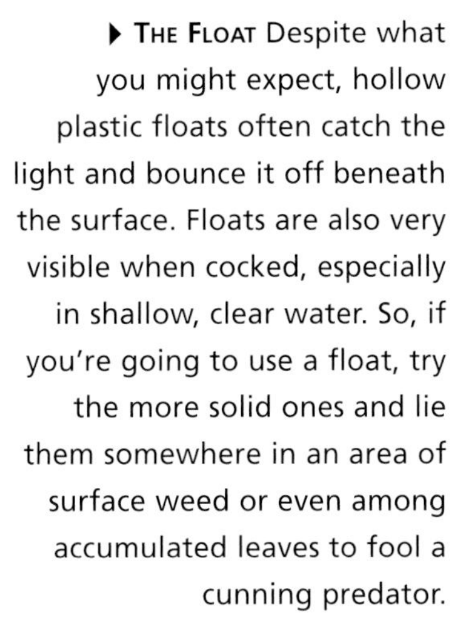

▸ The Float Despite what you might expect, hollow plastic floats often catch the light and bounce it off beneath the surface. Floats are also very visible when cocked, especially in shallow, clear water. So, if you're going to use a float, try the more solid ones and lie them somewhere in an area of surface weed or even among accumulated leaves to fool a cunning predator.

▸ Attractive Aromas This shot demonstrates why I like to use dead baits that have a good smell about them: the odours of the dead bait attract increasing numbers of small fish. A feeding frenzy takes place, and these ripples of excitement spread through the water and are picked up by big predators many yards away. Their instincts are aroused and they begin to follow the signals, homing in on the small fish and your bait.

THE PREDATOR AT HOME

Obviously, predators do roam in search of food, to spawn and in response to altered conditions, but many of them establish, at the very least, semi-permanent homes. I remember talking to renowned pike-angler Vic Bellars many years ago. He said that if you took a new barren pit of several acres in extent and introduced some pike and a fridge into it, virtually all the fish would be round the discarded machine within days. Any object acts like a magnet, offering a source of comfort in an otherwise featureless domain. Home to most predators is vitally important because they spend so much of their time there, waiting for their food to digest and the hunger pangs to pick up again. The best places are generally picked off by the bigger fish. For example, the sub-surface plateaux just off the coast in the Baltic Sea offer magnificent protection against the tides and currents and yet they're right in the middle of the migration routes for major prey species such as herring. Guess what? These prime homes are colonized by the biggest of the Baltic pike.

▲ **Sea Bass** These fish tend to have a large territory, but when they can seize the chance, they still enjoy the security of harbours where they can nestle behind timber piles or amid rocky crannies.

The Importance of Features

Features and structures are the two big words when it comes to plotting any water. Weed and reed beds, fallen trees and man-made influences (for example, sunken cars or boat piers) are specific features. Structure simply means a change in the lake bottom, either in the depth or in the material that makes up the bottom. Structure also includes such irregularities as points, plateaux, reefs, and channels. Up to ninety per cent of most waters is barren of fish, so how can you find the ten per cent heaving with fish life? Some anglers locate features using electronic aids and sonic fish-finders. On small waters, use Polaroids and, if possible, a boat. Don't overlook plumbing depths with rod, line and float. Watch other, more experienced, anglers and make a note of results. Some larger waters even have detailed charts.

MAN-MADE FEATURES Features are always important to fish, especially if they're found in an otherwise barren stretch of water. If the man-made features are near to a good structure, such as a drop-off, they become even more valuable. Here, a pipe in a dam proves a magnet for small fish, larger predators (bass) and even hunting terrapins!

REFUSE This old tyre was thrown into a stream, settling some 200 yards from the bridge from which it was thrown. After a year, it had bedded into the sandy bottom and was proving an absolute haven for minnows, gudgeon, bullhead and even crayfish. A large brown trout also took up residence in the shelter of the tyre and lived there for at least a couple of years. Today, a chub of around five pounds is an almost permanent resident.

◀ **Perch and Humans** Of all predatory species, perch are one of the most adaptable and are highly inquisitive. When I'm diving, they're one of the first species to come over and investigate, possibly for food, but more likely because they see me as a potential new home! The perch in this shot rarely strayed away from a group of old pots. What a boat angler rarely realizes is that, as soon as he drops an anchor, perch are very likely to shelter around the rope. The perch fisherman will frequently be casting yards out into the lake when the fish are actually beneath his rod tip!

▲ **Protective Cover** If perch can't find fridges, ropes or pottery, then the standard features that nature offers will have to do! Semi-permanent features, such as this fallen alder branch, provide most of what these small predators desire. Here a perch can lie up, shielded from the light, secure in a little cocoon of its own. It will venture out to feed and explore, but the alder fringe provides a bolt-hole in times of danger.

▶ **Tight Casting** Natural features don't come better than this – trees actually growing in water some five feet deep. The feature here is pretty well permanent, and gives excellent cover and shade from a burning sun. Moreover, it's positioned near a structure, a deep channel some four or five yards away from the tree roots. This shot was taken in Spain, with black bass in residence, but these could just as easily have been pike or perch. To get the very best out of this type of feature, pin-point casting is essential. Also, If you're moving into territory like this, you need the gear to back you up. Whatever your normal line strength is, double it in conditions like this. Even for a bass of three or four pounds, twenty-pound breaking strain is not over the top in these situations.

▶ **Slop** I love this American term because it describes precisely what you often come across when you're diving, especially in shallower water. What you'll find is a tangle of weed, perhaps roots, algae and the normal flotsam and jetsam of a typical water. The resulting combination is hard to define, but what it does provide is a piece of water that can be several degrees cooler than surrounding areas. As a diver, you can physically feel this, and in very hot conditions you will find pike holed up in such areas.

◀ **Weeds** There are numerous types of weed, including floating weeds, submerged weeds and emerging weeds. The bulrush family, famously, has over fifty different members. Some weeds are good, others less so, and it takes practice to differentiate. You can't go far wrong, though, with emergent reeds such as bulrushes. Tench adore grubbing around bulrush roots, and most predatory species enjoy the safety provided by a big colony of these reeds.

▲ **The Living Shelter** Living bushes or trees in water can be particularly attractive. The leaves attract any number of insects that, naturally enough, fall off into the water and provide food for both predators and prey fish. If the predators are fortunate, birds might be nesting in a living tree, and a nest brings the constant hope of an over-ambitious fledgling. Leaves also give extra shade during the heat of the summer, and, of course, because the tree is not dead or dying, it offers much more promise as a permanent residence.

▸ **Fishing the Tangle** You are always going to find predators in tangled areas like this, but to fish close in calls for very accurate casting. Consider shorter rods and easy-to-use, precision multipliers. Also, work on your underhand casting: you're not banging a bait to the horizon here, but simply flicking it into tight, promising areas. Make every cast work as hard as possible, and consider how you can draw a lure back parallel to weed beds to get maximum efficiency all the time.

▲ **Portraying the Prey** If the predators that you are after are wise, it's often necessary to present accurate imitations of their natural food items. These sticklebacks are typical: they've taken up residence in a weedy area with many branches, but they are preyed upon by smaller pike and perch. Tiny plugs and flies or, perhaps, convincing jigs are the baits to fish areas such as these with. You might also need to buy weedless hooks, which have a wire guard to resist snagging. Failing that, if you cut the lead hook from a treble you'll pick up considerably less weed than with all three points protruding.

Down in the Cabbage Patch

If you can find a truly big feature then you're onto a real winner: more prey fish are likely to be attracted to it, and that means a build up of predators. For example, a cabbage patch provides fairly constant cover for over a hundred yards of river. They are mammoth features that will have been present for years, and work as a magnet for huge numbers of fish. It's a wonderland of light and shade. There are cool areas and places where the current above is almost completely deflected. The cabbages are also very food-rich. As a further inducement, the cabbages look difficult to fish, and this tends to deter anglers. Even in winter, when temperatures drop and the cabbages die away, the area remains a focus: there's still plenty of cover for fish down there in the bottom zone as the flood waters thunder above.

▲ **Greedy Browsers** This is a perfect area for roach, probably the pike's preferred food item in this river. The roach know the pike are a danger, even in this underwater forest, but the advantages of the cabbages outweigh the menace. Snails, beetles, caddis, shrimp... virtually every primary food source for the roach is available in large quantities. Winter or summer, the cabbage patch provides a constant larder that the roach shoals find hard to resist.

▶ **Deep Diving** If pike are hunting, the roach will be restless and skittery. Here the roach are feeding well and all is serene. The pike are lying doggo and you need to do something drastic to get their attention. A big-lipped deep diver may work. You'll have to cast short and tight and let it dig down in short bursts. At the very least, an aggressive plug like this will cause a disturbance and stir matters up somewhat.

▶ **Work Shallow** If the cabbages are proving too much of a problem deeper down, you'll have to look at a lure that works either on the surface or just beneath it. There's every chance, anyway, that your deep diver has already done its work and stirred a pike or two into some sort of action. Here the aroused pike is looking closely at a shallow-worked plug.

▶ **Injured Fish** When you look at this shot of a roach with its newly punctured flesh, you realize that the cabbages are almost like a fish factory. This is where the roach and the pike both earn their living on a constant day-to-day basis. This roach soon succumbed to a disease around its injured area and, as its speed declined, it was quickly taken by a pike.

The Sea Scene

One of the beauties of lure gear is that it unlocks virtually every door in the fishing world. You can catch carp on lures, as well as predators. You can travel to nearly every country in the world with your lure kit and know you will get some rod-bending action. Nowadays, a lot of freshwater lure anglers are trying out the sea scene with ever-increasing success. The oceans might appear to be big places, but the same rules still apply. Providing you understand the fish and can read the water in front of you, then you're unlikely to be casting into a fishless void. Undoubtedly, however, the place to start your seawater lure fishing is close in, especially around man-made features such as harbours, jetties, piers and so on. This is where many species of fish like to explore, and this is where plugs, spoons, spinners and jigs can be worked with confidence.

▲ **Using Cover** Harbours, marinas, jetties – anywhere with boats, you will find fish. Smaller fish love the shade that the boats give them from light and from winged predators, and the fish that feed on them come in close to enjoy the harvest. Before fishing in boat areas, ensure that angling is allowed, as certain places are off limits. Also, look carefully at the skein of anchor ropes: let a fish get round those and it's lost for good. Many of these places tend to be busy during the daytime, so you are well advised to get out as early as possible in the morning or stay on after the light is fading.

▸ **Unusual Features** These fingerlings are gathering around shards of ancient Roman pottery – a perfect example of how man's influence along the shoreline can attract fish. Pilings, sea defences, slipways, promenades and piers are just a handful of the ways in which mankind has helped to concentrate fish stocks. For the committed boat fisherman, offshore wrecks have served exactly the same purpose.

▲ **The Mackerel Season** If you're starting out as a lure angler on the sea, you just won't find more fun than the obliging mackerel. They haunt most coasts during the summer, and frequently swim close inshore. Moreover, you can fish for them with comparatively light gear... freshwater tackle and seven- or eight-pound line should be strong enough. Try a small silver spinner with, perhaps, a little red wool round the tail treble. Get to a good vantage point, such as a rocky headland, and keep casting, waiting for the fish to come to you; or you can travel light, keep on the move and search out the fish yourself.

RUBBER JIGS

Rubber jigs... just what are we talking about here? Well, there's no mystery or magic involved; simply lures fashioned out of rubber to resemble any one of a number of living creatures. The method has been highly developed throughout the USA, Scandinavia and Eastern and Central Europe. The South Africans, moreover, believe that if a creature lives in the water then it can be caught on rubber.

Rubber jigs come in a bewildering variety of sizes, shapes, colours and actions. You will find virtually any living food form imitated – fish, worms, crabs, frogs, crayfish, crickets, sand eels, prawns, squid and any wiggly grub that you can imagine. So, what's the best way to start? Perhaps the best way forward is to invest in one of the 'big bait buckets' that many operations offer. You'll be presented with a true Aladdin's Cave of rubber jigs of all sorts. Then it's up to you to get down to experimenting and thinking your way through to the core of this hugely productive method.

▲ **A Proud Man** This stunning pike was taken on a shad-type rubber jig in the shallows early one spring morning; it had probably just spawned, was hungry and was looking around for an easy meal.

Success in the Baltic

The efficiency of rubber baits was brought home to me some four years ago when fishing in the Baltic Sea with my great friend Johnny Jensen and our two excellent Swedish guides. It was a bright, late April day off the Swedish coastline and I, as normal, fished my array of plugs. I landed one fish, a pike of around six pounds. The two Swedes and Johnny tried a variety of rubbers and they landed some sixty-odd fish between them. The next day was much the same. Once more, I fished my plugs and spinners to virtually no avail while a steady stream of good pike fell to my companions. It was late that second day when I finally admitted defeat and switched to rubbers myself. The lesson was clear: rubbers can be utterly fantastic – but you've still got to learn how to use them.

▲ **Furious Attack** Rising temperatures, clear water and hungry, aggressive pike... an ideal combination for using rubber jigs. However, they can still be adapted to working in colder, murkier water – but more of that later. This particular fish took very close to the boat, indeed, and you'll often find with rubbers that pike will stalk them for a long time before making a final decision. The answer is obviously to work the lure right to your very feet before removing it for another cast.

◀ **Finally Subdued** This same fish eventually glides towards the boat, but only after four or five powerful, snaking runs. Truly, those two days with Johnny, Pers and Hakken were an eye-opener. What did they teach me? Location, location, location. My colleagues spent ages deciding on each and every move around the bays. Part of the time was spent studying an echo sounder, looking especially for plateaux surrounded by deep drop-offs. Failing that, they would search out the thickest, most watery of reed beds. Also, their casting was just that little bit more specific than mine when I, too, took to the rubber. Perhaps I was afraid of over-casting and losing the lure, or maybe I wasn't quite used to the weight and flight through the air, but each and every cast of theirs was landing absolutely on the reed fringe, whereas mine generally fell a foot or two short. That difference appeared to be absolutely crucial.

◀ **A Fine Fish** Pers certainly deserved this fish. To watch him work a lure was absolutely extraordinary. In fact, it was almost an exact imitation of fly fishing, in that he spent every second analyzing the movement of his jig, just as a nymph master is constantly aware of what the fly is doing as it nears the trout. Pers would watch, hawk-eyed, as the lure fell through the water, watching for any twitch of the line that would signal a take on the drop. He would then leave it on the bottom, 100 per cent alert to any sign that the motionless lure had been picked up. Then, the retrieve would be immaculate – sometimes a twitch, sometimes just a stammer of the rod tip. Then a bit of a spurt so that the rubber would rise and then flutter down again in an irresistible fashion.

Imitating Nature

On a recent trip to Spain we came across a colossal gathering of large-mouth bass, one of the most absorbing of all predators. We tried every type of fly imaginable. Nothing. Spinners? Nothing. Small plugs? I'll swear they laughed. Only when we put on a small, rubber imitation of a crayfish did things began to happen.

That's one of the great things about rubber lures: there are just so many different colours, shapes and sizes, representing so many different aquatic creatures that you're never going to run out of options. There's always another trick left up your sleeve, another rubber untried in the box. This is the important thing: open your mind to the whole concept and you will discover some fascinating fishing.

▲ **The Crayfish** There aren't many predatory species that won't gobble up a crayfish if they happen to see one stranded and out in the open. Even those menacing, click-clacking claws won't dissuade a hungry fish from dinner. Watch crayfish in the wild – this is the key to successful rubber fishing. Stumble through the shallows, picking up stones, chasing the crayfish, watching how they hide and then how they scuttle backwards to avoid detection or capture. That's how you should work your rubber imitation. Always try to mimic the natural as carefully as you can. So, let the rubber fall to the bottom, leave it there a while and then twitch it backwards at great speed for a foot or so before letting it settle, hopefully as naturally as possible, in a rocky crevice.

◀ **Sinking** Newts are eagerly devoured by virtually every fish that swims. Of course, you wouldn't use a real newt any more than you would a real crayfish, but this is where rubbers come into their own. Newts spend a lot of time on the bottom, usually close to cover. Sometimes the downward journey will be very slow, arms and legs outstretched, simply hovering to the bottom, presumably trying to escape detection. Watch and consider, and then set up your rubber to match their behaviour.

▲ **Up It Comes** Try to choose a rubber that matches the colours and sizes of the newts that you're seeing. Some have yellow stomachs, some greenish and some orange. Try them all until you hit a winning combination, and then work that rubber just like the real creature. Cast it out and let it sink slowly to the bottom, perhaps with an odd twitch on the way down. Let it rest there a minute or two, just flicking it from time to time to send off a puff of silt. When they need air, newts come to the top as quickly as possible and take a gulp before drifting back down again, so bring the rubber to the surface in quick, sharp thrusts. Repeat the process and watch the line intently for any sign of a take. Remember, it's always important to fit a wire trace just in case there are pike or zander about.

▶ **Baby Snakes** It's surprising just how many snakes there are in and around the waterside. In Spain, I've frequently watched baby adders trying to cross coves and bays just off the main river. Believe me, there aren't many that make it. They swim on the surface, head held high, in a lazy S-type motion, sending out enticing ripples on either side. With a floating rubber this action is, once again, not difficult to imitate. With most rubber jigs, a single hook will do. However, when using something longer, perhaps to imitate a small snake or a sand eel, it's sometimes useful to include a two-hook rig.

▶ **Minnows on the Move** Once again, watch how these prey creatures are behaving. They hover and then move in short bursts – exactly the motion you need to give your lures. There's no shortage of rubbers made to look and behave like a small fish, one of the preferred predator targets; but when you use them, your hook-up rig is absolutely vital. You've not only got to choose the right rig but also put the hook in so that the action is as realistic as possible. It often pays to fill a bath with water or use a garden pond before setting out. Set up a good number of rigs and look at them closely in clear, shallow conditions and make as many amendments as necessary to achieve the perfect action.

Triggering the Senses

With rubber lures, the whole idea is to appeal to the senses, so you're looking for a rubber that has the right colour, shape and feel, perhaps with a smell and certainly with an appealing movement. This is where very careful jig choice and experimentation in visible water comes in. Colour is an interesting issue: what are the considerations? Perhaps you're looking to match the colour of the jig with the food type it's trying to represent. Perhaps you're looking for something visible in cloudy water. Shape is all-important, along with size. Once again, you're initially trying to imitate a known, desirable food item – or are you? There may be times when you want to introduce something that the fish feel threatened or angered by and will attack with hostility. Again, rubber fishing gives you these options.

◀ **AFLOAT** If you can, get a boat. A boat gives you a huge advantage for two main reasons. Firstly, it leaves you free to explore much more water and to find the perfect location, often far from the bank or close to otherwise unapproachable reed beds. Secondly, the closer you are to your fish and the shorter your casts, the greater your control. Also, with less line out, there's a greater chance that you'll pick up on a delicate, subtle take.

◀ **THE SET-UP** I wasn't very happy with some aspects of the set-up used by this angler as he rubber fished a deep, relatively clear river. For my liking, the snap link was far too large and clumsy. His response was that he was after big fish and he didn't want to take any risks. I have to admit that the rubbers looked attractive from below and did work, so I guess that what may look all wrong from the bank can, in fact, pass muster beneath.

Movement Motion gives the rubber that suggestion of life. Sometimes a single tail, like the one we've just seen, will be enough, but there are other occasions when a twin tail will make all the difference, as this exaggerates the movement. Twin tails catch the light more and glitter dramatically, and sometimes this extra dash is exactly what's needed.

Smell Notice the large eye on this rubber – a great attack target for the predator to focus on. Make no mistake, many predators will follow rubbers very closely, get right up to them and deliberate long and hard before taking them. I believe that smell can be important in the final decision. Try dipping lures in a powdered flavour for added attraction. Failing that, keep them well-coated or injected with fish oil.

Feel-Good Factor Rubber jigs score when it comes to texture, too, and this is where they triumph over plugs made of wood, plastic or metal. Many predators will actually suck the rubber and spit it out again once or twice before making a final decision. Large-mouthed bass are very prone to this, as are large perch. You can even let a rubber lie motionless on the bottom, like this, and curious predators will take.

▲ CONSERVATION Catching fish is good fun, but their conservation must be top priority. Rubber baits are so attractive, they're often gulped right down, especially by large-mouthed species, such as pike, so to avoid harming the fish, follow a few simple rules. Use single hooks if you can, and if you can't, go for fine-wire trebles. Keep the tension on during the fight and you won't lose any fish. As for kit, always have long-nosed pliers with you, and a set of mini bolt croppers to cut your trebles free if necessary. This rubber is fitted with a barbless single, so I will have no worries about unhooking.

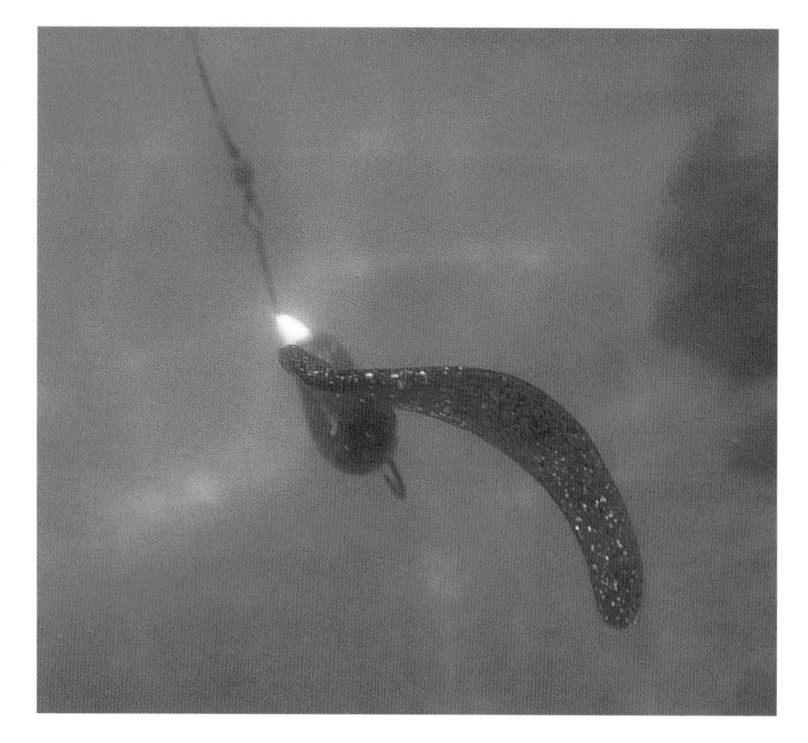

◀ BE AWARE OF TEMPERATURE If you are going to take rubber fishing seriously – as you really should – it's a good idea to take a thermometer with you as all rubbers behave differently when the water temperature goes either up or down. Some rubbers, for example, go rigid and hardly work at all. Others achieve near meltdown! This is one of my favourites, with a great action in warm water. To find out exactly what your rubbers will do under different conditions, use the humble, domestic bath. Try every temperature, test your lures and note the results.

▶ **Rubber Action** The tail of this rubber twitches in an irresistible fashion at a certain speed, and you, the angler, need to know this if you're going to make it behave like an escaping newt or worm. Still at the bath side, sort your rubbers out into different classifications, from violent action to subdued motion, and pull each one through the water to see how it reacts in still water. Try all sorts of hooking arrangements and hook sizes. Vary the weight of the lead head, or go for a weighted hook. To see how the rubber works when it's hooked up and in a current, your shower head will come in handy. Place it under the bath water, switch it on and, lo and behold, you've got a ready-made current to test your hooked-up rubber.

impart movement through the rod tip

try to achieve a rippling motion in the water

allow the jig to hit bottom

Working the Jig

Really concentrate on working the jig and making it appear as life-like as possible. Vary the speed of the retrieve and move the rod tip up and down and from side to side. It's a good idea to let the jig hit bottom every now and then so that puffs of silt come up, giving an impression of a small fish trying to escape or a crayfish burrowing under a rock. Experiment with different coloured jig tails and actions. Work the jig right back to the rod tip: takes often come at the last critical moment.

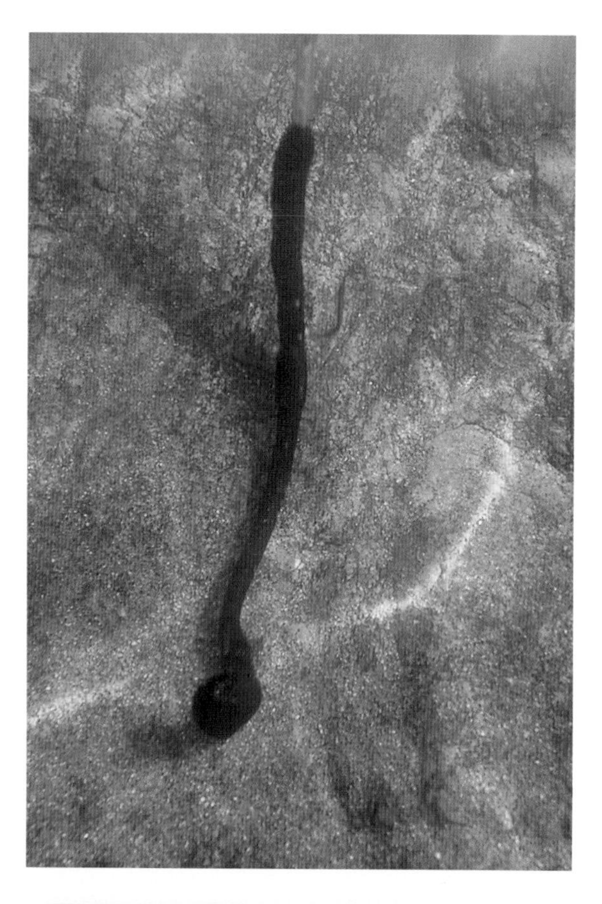

◀ **Positioning** Yet another advantage of being on a boat when the water is clear, the light is bright and you're wearing good Polaroids is that you can see the bottom topography clearly. It's one thing to work the right lure in an enticing way but it's also important to think about the exact route that the rubber will take. See how this worm is being crawled up a stone wall in the most natural of ways.

▼ **Proportions** This rubber looks far too large for the immature perch that has been attracted to it, but if you know that perch can swallow prey a third of their body weight, it begins to make more sense. However, look at the bottom vegetation – dead alders and leaves – the start of the winter. Water temperatures have plummeted and no predator is likely to want to charge around after its prey. This is where a slowly worked rubber comes in – you can give a predator plenty of time to look and make up its mind.

Speed of Movement As temperatures drop, fish become more finicky and less eager to chase a dramatically working rubber that swings around in wide arcs. Instead, go for something more subdued that can be worked in a subtle, yet convincing fashion. At this time of the year – onset of winter – it's vital to know the sink rate of your jig. Ensure that you know how long it takes to fall a yard through the water, and count it down so you know the depth you're fishing over. In cold conditions, predators are likely to be closer to the bottom, so if you work that zone success is more likely. This rubber gets down quickly, so it's ideal for working the bed.

The Fluidity of the Fly It may not be a rubber, but big flies like this have a great deal in common with rubber jigs because, once again, they have a truly natural action. It's no wonder that flies made of fur and feather catch so many more trout on all-method fisheries than do spinners or plugs. There's something about the rush of water through the hackles and the trapped bubbles of oxygen that give them a real fishy feel. Once you've discovered the advantages of rubbers, you've got to try flies, as they can imitate nature equally closely.

Going for Bass

If you live in northern Europe and you haven't yet fished for black bass, then you really should. You'll soon see why the Americans and Spanish are absolutely wild about them. They look nice and fight well, but, above all, they're the most cheeky, inquisitive, canny and downright infuriating predators that you're ever likely to come up against. They don't grow that big – three or four pounds is a good weight for a large-mouth – but that's not the point. As a challenge, these fish are the ultimate. I've fished for bass in the USA, but most of my bass fishing has been in Spain, so I have to admit that my own experiences are restricted to warm weather bassing. The fish may be active during these warmer months, but they're certainly not stupid. I've also been fortunate that my introduction to bass has been made through several highly talented Spanish friends, including Rafa, who has proved to be enthusiastic, skilful and free with his advice.

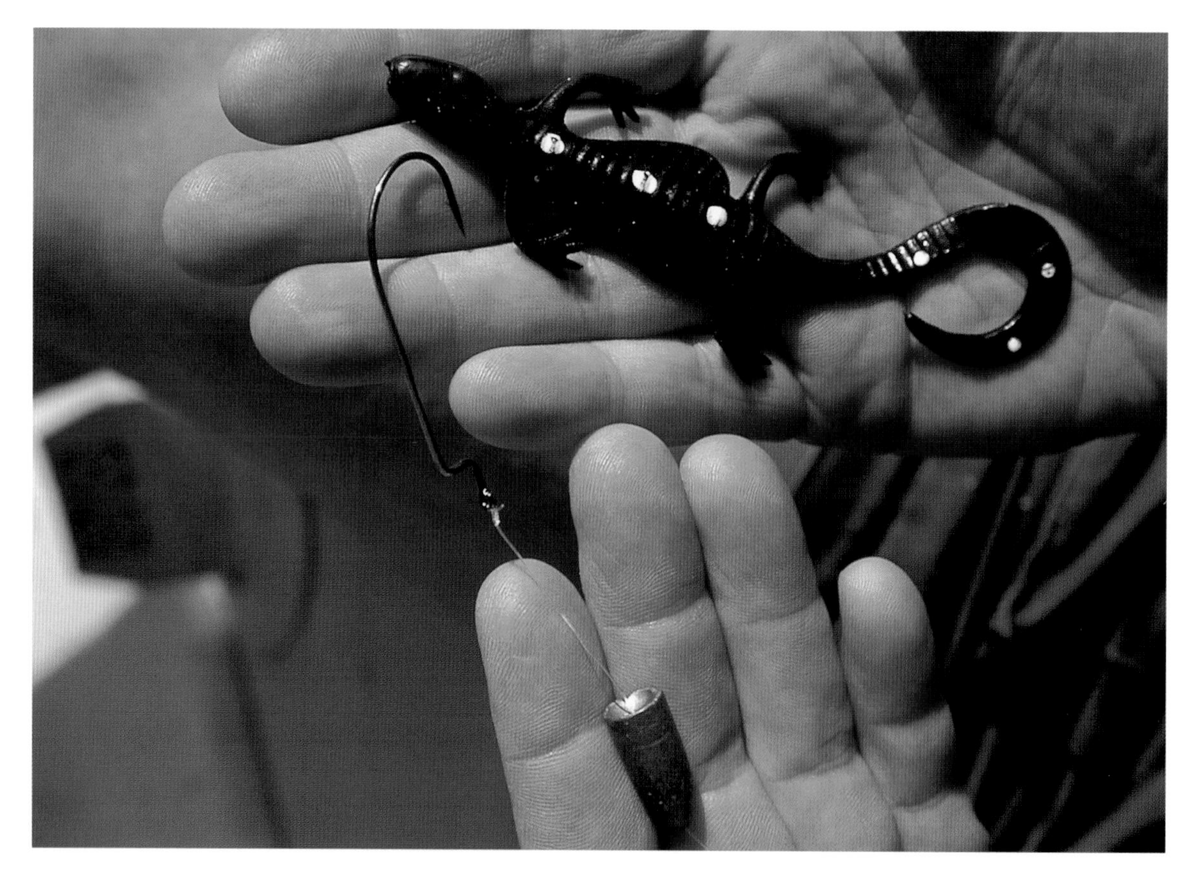

▲ TACKLE CHOICE The wide variety of aquatic life in Spain gives the angler a wide choice of rubbers. There are water snakes, crayfish, all manner of very large creepy-crawly nymphs and endless types of small fish. Lizards abound, and a black rubber such as the one pictured here can't go far wrong. A boat is imperative, with a large engine to get you swiftly from one location to another on the big waters. Once you're close, use oars to waft you soundlessly over the hotspots.

▸ **What the Line Tells You** If you fish in shallow, clear water, you will be able to watch the bass's reaction to the rubber lures. Generally, however, you'll be fishing quite deep, especially in bright conditions like this when the bass won't come far from the rocks. Once you lose sight of your rubber, then it's your line that tells you everything – when your rubber hits bottom, how it's working (to some degree) and certainly when a fish is showing interest. A take can come at anytime – when the rubber is on the way down, static on the bottom, twitched along the bottom or as it's being retrieved. Notice how delicately Rafa is holding the line, feeling for any indication of a take.

▸ **A Fine Bass Taken on a Rubber** Rafa made a good, long cast, kept the line tight and caused the lure to sink in an arc towards him. The lure's tail would have been working all the way to the bottom. Once it hit the bottom, Rafa let it rest there for a while to allow the bass to move in and investigate. The odd twitch of the rod tip made the bass curious, then a sharp upward stroke kicked the rubber fish into life. He worked the lure in a sink-and-draw fashion, keeping in constant contact. He let the rubber touch bottom and then immediately flicked it up... bang, the result is there for all to see.

Jigging the Reed Beds

The action takes place in a bay just off the Baltic Sea. I've been dropped off in a very large, shallow bay where there are plenty of reeds but with a lot of open water between them – perfect both for lurking pike and for working a rubber. It's earlier in the year this time, water temperatures are lower and the pike probably haven't all spawned. In all probability, there are still some big females very close to the shore, searching for small but select groups of males with whom to cavort. When you consider there are fish well into the forty-pound mark, it makes for exciting sport!

▲ **Hybrid Rubber** When the water is cool, it often pays to go for a hybrid rubber. For example, take the marriage of a wooden jerk bait with a large rubber curly tail. The curly tail sinks quite quickly, perhaps too fast for a lethargic pike. The jerk bait, on the other hand, is wooden and therefore more buoyant. Together, the two sink slowly in an enticing fashion, and the combination can be painstakingly worked to look very much like a wounded fish. In this instance, Pers recommended a normal rubber fish set-up, but one light enough not to plummet straight to the bottom.

▸ **Up Close** There are times when any lure fished on the bottom can be enticing. You can kick up puffs of silt that attract a pike's attention and trigger the predatory instinct. The sparkle of sunlight on the lure can help, but sometimes it's just a bit too much. In bright conditions, a totally black rubber, which creates a threatening silhouette, can be taken with real force.

▸ **Success** I don't like too long a rod when it comes to rubber fishing for pike. Something in the eight- to nine-and-a-half-foot range is about right. However, there's no such thing as a general-purpose lure rod – you have ultra-light fishing at one end of the scale and the demanding jerk baiting at the other. You need to consider the weight of the lures that you will be casting and the action of the blank to make them work properly. The best that I can recommend is a specialized lure rod from a reputable company – the Shimano Technium is a good example.

SURFACE POPPING

Top-water lure fishing is arguably the most exciting way to catch a predator. Pike, chub, bass, asp and several members of the salmon family all take greedily from the surface. So, too, will perch and even zander if conditions are spot on. Basically, surface lures fall into a number of specific categories. First of all, there are crawlers that swim with a wobbling action. Then there are the chuggers that come in different sizes and shapes, but which all rely on a concave front, rather like a mouth, to give them their action and sound. Next come stick baits, which are rather nondescript and totally dependent on the angler to give them life. Fourthly, you have the prop baits – top-water plugs that have up to three lightweight propeller blades mounted on them. Then, there are the others – anything that makes a bit of a disturbance on the surface can catch the eye of a hungry predator if conditions are right. Believe me, there's no more dynamic or intimate way to fish.

▲ **Lurking** All predators, pike especially, often slide into the shallow margins to sunbathe and to investigate a potentially rich feeding zone. A pike that looks relatively comatose can soon explode into life.

Surface Considerations

Begin your surface lure fishing when conditions are at their best. Firstly, vitally, the water needs to be quiet. You don't want the intrusion of boats, water-skiers, swimmers or anything else that's going to ruin the serenity of the water. Next on the check list is water temperature. In the northern hemisphere, most top-water work is best done from late spring to early autumn. Wherever you are in the world, there's probably not going to be a huge amount of surface activity until the water reaches 20°C or so. Look to the shallow margins first, because this is where the water is at its warmest and you're more likely to get some action. Water clarity is another important consideration; it's much more difficult to see a lure on the top if the water is cloudy. Quiet, still, warm, clear water is just about the ideal.

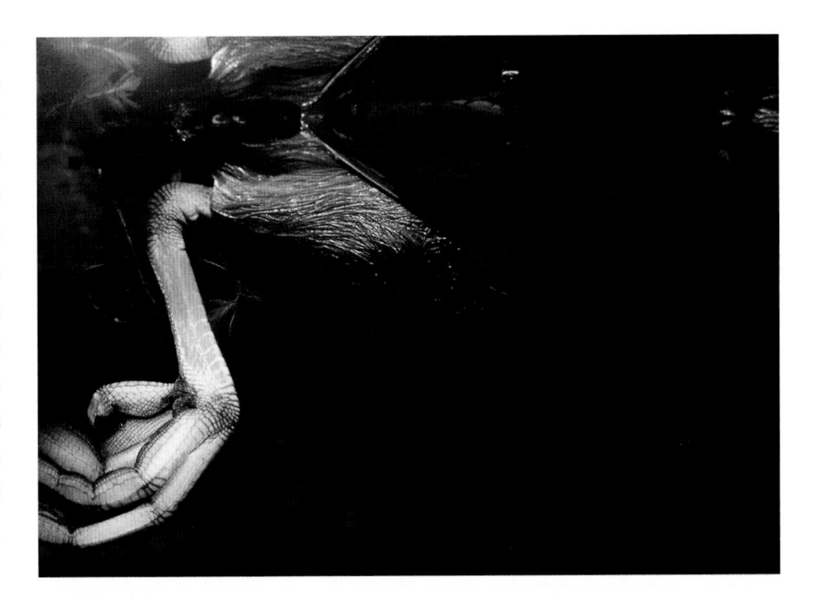

▶ **TANTALIZING** Any predator worth his salt will always have a beady eye on the surface for any titbit that may come his way. Mature coots are pretty well safe from all but the biggest of pike, but the flash of light on their webbed feet and lower plumage can provide powerful stimuli. Also, pike frequently hang around areas being worked by coots because they flush out toads, frogs and small fish from the weed beds.

▶ **IRRESISTIBLE** Mammals, such as this water vole, are certainly well within the range of many predators, and definitely pike from just a couple of pounds upwards. The shallows offer all manner of goodies from above. Fledgling birds, for example, that fall from the nest can prove particularly attractive. You'd be surprised at the size of some of the predators that come into very shallow water.

The Story of a Mouse

When you're doing something a little bit different, such as surface fishing, you come to realize that not all the rules have been formulated, and that you can break a bit of new ground. So it was with me when two things coincided: firstly, I was sent some imitation mouse patterns to try out and, secondly, I found a clutch of small- to medium-sized pike in the shallow, almost stagnant, water of a local river. It was too good an opportunity to miss, but it took me a good while to work out a winning approach. One problem I had was that the fish just weren't hungry: many small roach and perch inhabit this stretch of river and the pike, though interested in the mouse, had no need to fight over it. That's an important point: the hungrier the pike are, the more likely they are to go for your surface lures.

◀ **Seen from Above** Given that stick baits just look like a piece of kindling, it's easy to think that your surface lure doesn't have to be very realistic, but I'd disagree with that. Something that looks very much alive puts you one step ahead of the game. However, even a creation like this, with its enticing wiggly tail, needs a good deal of angler input. It's just not enough to cast out any surface bait and pull it back without consideration.

◀ **Seen from Below** You might imagine that all a pike sees of a lure from below is a black silhouette with ripples leading from it, but when I dive in very shallow water, then I, at least, do see colour: perhaps not as much as I would with a lure at eye level, but from a distance you can certainly tell whether a creation is green, blue or yellow, for example. So, if you're not getting takes, and you've tried everything else, a change of colour might prove to be the key to success.

▸ **Showing Interest** It was quite obvious that pike could pick up the presence of the mouse from anything up to ten yards away. They certainly weren't seeing the mouse at that sort of distance but were, in fact, picking up the vibrations it transmitted. These vibrations stimulated interest, and the pike would frequently glide from quite surprising distances to investigate the disturbance.

▸ **Taking a Closer Look** A pike shows interest, glides into the area, spurts up to the mouse but then just stops and watches. In my experience, unless the pike are seriously hungry, they'll very rarely take any surface lure if they can have a good look at it. Sometimes you can stimulate them into an attack by letting the surface lure hang for a few seconds before twitching it into a fast retrieve. If that retrieve is towards weed beds, so much the better – the pike will fear it is making its escape.

◀ **Ignored** The pike has now moved away and that's the end of that. What could I have done? Well, perhaps night fishing is the answer. A calm, warm, clear night often sees pike crashing in the shallows as they feed. Perhaps I should also have worked the mouse with more care and consideration. Always work that lure, whatever it is you're using, as slowly as possible. This gives the pike time to intercept it and make an attack. Also, if the lure is moving slowly the pike can focus that attack more accurately. Many attacks are not struck because the pike has actually missed the lure.

▲ **A Change of Tactics** After a couple of failed sessions, a move to a mini, ultra-light plug like this one may prove more successful. These are not much bigger than a large postage stamp and they're my standard approach to difficult predators if other techniques aren't working. They're particularly useful for smaller waters with plenty of reeds and lots of nooks and crannies, as you can work them very accurately and really search waters intimately. You can still work them as surface poppers, but do it slowly, or they tend to spin and lose control.

Tempting a Taiman

Top-water lure fishing is certainly a method that travels – peacock bass in Bolivia; musky fishing in North America; asp on the River Volga; black bass in Spain or Florida; barramundi in the brackish backwaters of Australia and, famously, the huge predatory taiman of Central Asia. It's long been known that taiman are particularly attracted into the shallows at night where they will eat mice, lemmings and, especially, marmots as they attempt a river crossing. In fact, so voracious can taiman be at the surface that they've been known to attack anything from a floating dead squirrel to a child's teddy bear! Taiman are big, hungry and, generally, completely uneducated, but that doesn't mean that they're easy to deceive. All the usual rules of surface plug fishing need to be applied.

▶ **Dawn is Best** On most waters and for most predators, surface popping is at its most efficient at dawn. This is when predators seem to be most active in the margins. Also, consider trying at dusk and well into the night. All evidence suggests that it's during the periods of half-light that predators are really at work.

▶ **Crystal Clear** Most northerly Mongolian rivers run crystal clear, at least until they disgorge into Siberia. This means that your surface lure has to be as convincing as you can make it. This particular mouse pattern looks good, both from above and, vitally, from below.

◀ **Zeroing In** Is there a more exciting sight in predator fishing than watching a big predator home in on its prey? Taiman are big fish, so I suggest using mono of around forty pounds breaking strain. When you're casting these surface lures a long way, especially on short rods, there's a lot of pressure on the line, and you don't want a break-off. Also, as you're plying your surface plugs so close to snags, you will often have to put extreme pressure on a big, angry fish to keep it out of trouble. Once again, to leave a plug in a fish is unforgivable. Moreover, if you do hook up, you stand much more chance of retrieving that expensive lure if you can really give it some solid heave-ho.

◀ **The Critical Moment** How do you make a big predator that has seen your top-water lure go in for the kill? If a bait is in open water like this, work it towards cover or the bank so that the predator thinks it's making its escape. Try this trick: take in a short amount of line, say a foot or two, pause, then almost instantly move the rod tip up and backwards. This makes the bait rise up in the water and, as you wind again, it will settle back down. This action proves devastating with all big predators.

Third Time Lucky Pike aren't the only predators to miss the lure on occasion. This taiman took three attempts to hit a plug worked across the surface close to a weed bed, by which time the lucky angler had almost overdosed on adrenalin. With its powerful body and broad tail, a fish like this can put up quite a fight in rocky, fast-flowing Mongolian waters.

On the Move There are occasions when it can pay to work a single fish over and over with a top-water lure, but this is not the norm. Generally, you're much better keeping on the move, investigating new water and putting your lures over fresh fish. In Mongolia, the water is virtually limitless, and it's not unusual to walk twenty miles a day. Travel as light as you can: rod, reel, traces, pack of lures, net and, if you wish, camera and off you go.

The Take A twenty-pound taiman sucks in a large streamer fly from the surface. Streamer flies really do work for big predators, and taiman are just as eager for them as pike. Real satisfaction comes with using them on fly tackle that is designed for the job, but you can get away with employing an ordinary rod and line providing you've got some weight to help casting.

The Fall of a Chub

When you're lure fishing for chub in flowing water, it generally pays to go for the smaller lures. You'll also find the fish obligingly coming to the surface during the summer months. (In the winter, when diving, I generally chance upon them down deep.) Most of the surface lure types will take chub, providing they're reasonably small. With chub, it's vital to keep changing the model. Chub get wary very quickly, indeed, and once they've rejected a lure, they won't come again. For that reason, keep on the move and look for fresh fish. You will almost always find chub in and around snags, and your casting must be absolutely precise. Drop a surface plug more than a foot or so out of the critical zone and you can guarantee it will be ignored. Make sure, then, that you've got the gear for pin-point casting.

◀ **Look for Structure** If the water that you're fishing has little in the way of bankside vegetation, then you've got to look for structures under the water, and this is where rocks come in. Chub use these for shelter from the current and also as prolific feeding grounds. Even when you're only after chub, don't go too light on line – I would never go less than ten pounds breaking strain – and use a wire trace in case a pike or zander takes the lure.

◀ **Movement** Chub are amongst the wariest of all predators, and on small, clear waters it often pays to approach them from below. Cast a lure upstream and let it sweep across the current, bobbing along the surface, while you twitch it. Once the lure nears the chub, give a few sharp turns of the reel and the lure should dip beneath the surface like this. The action is something that chub find difficult to resist.

▸ **Know Your River** Time spent observing from the river bank is time well spent. Put on your Polaroids, a pair of waders and creep along the bank to build up a picture of where the fish are and how they are behaving. Here you see the surface lure giving a killing impression of light and life, and hopefully sparking a chub into the attack.

▸ **A Beauty** When it comes to experimenting with lures for chub, try mouse patterns, frog patterns or, very exciting, imitation grasshoppers. Crayfish patterns also work, as do all manner of bumblebee and beetle imitations. If these don't work, try going for one of the miniature crank baits that led to the downfall of this fish – the sound that these give out is important, so experiment.

Working the Water

Think very hard about the stretch of water and put your lure into all likely places, especially those close to snags. It's a good idea to cast two or three times to the same spot and to retrieve along the same line. Sometimes the first cast only alerts the fish to a possible meal and on the next retrieve it's actually prepared and ready to take. Pinpoint casting is best achieved with a short rod, say six to eight feet long. Don't flog a piece of water; travel light so you can search a stretch and then move on.

work the lure under bankside cover

direction of wind

search out weed beds

let the lure bounce the rocks

cast into rocky areas

cast in a radial pattern

Popping for Bass

Bass are very receptive to surface lures and will accept all the traditional types previously mentioned. Surface lures work best in calm water, especially in the mornings and evenings when the water is warm. A ripple definitely interests a fish. Bass can be the most infuriating of all predators and will frequently follow surface lures without striking. You will see the wake, but there won't be the take. What do you do? Try stopping the retrieve and letting the lure rest for a short while – four or five seconds ought to do the trick – then twitch it violently. Not every bass take is explosive – some can come up behind the lure and sip it in like a trout taking a buzzer. Top-water lures are particularly useful when your bass are deep in thick beds of vegetation and weed, as often only surface commotion can attract them out into open water.

◀ **EL DORADO** This is a shot of my favourite large-mouth bass water, a vast reservoir hidden in the mountains of Spain. It has all the features that a bass angler will recognize: shallow bays and deep drop-offs; stream mouths entering the reservoir through extensive reed beds; dramatic underwater structures; overhanging trees; man-made structures such as a water tower and a dam; plenty of small fish, but not so many that the bass aren't keen for that extra titbit.

◀ **PATIENCE** Cast your top lure out and leave it for a good few seconds, to let it settle. Sometimes bass will hit a lure as it bobs on the surface, or even when it's motionless. Tell-tale ripples also attract the bass. This is why it's so important to make the accuracy of the cast paramount. The closer you can get it into the snag-infested area that bass adore, the more chance you have of a take.

▸ **The Jerk** After five or even ten seconds, begin the retrieve with a violent jerk that sends an explosive message out across the water. You'll hear the lure as it chugs and sends up bubbles. So, too, will the bass. After an initial jerk like this, it often pays to stop winding and let the lure bob there for a couple of seconds before beginning a more traditional retrieve.

▸ **The Rip** There are times when you've just got to rip a top lure across the surface to make a real commotion, sending out lots of noise and ripples. This can pull two or more bass into the area. If you're using a propeller bait, it may pay to experiment with the blades themselves. If you bend them backwards, they'll sometimes clip the lure and make even more of a commotion.

▸ **Definite Take** There's no doubt whatsoever that this bass wanted the surface lure! Sometimes, they will hammer into a lure with such ferocity that the attack heaves them clear of the water. Once the fish is hooked, keep the pressure on. Almost certainly there will be more jumps to come, especially as the bass nears the bank. Be prepared, and don't be caught out giving the fish slack line, or the lure is likely to be thrown.

◀ **The Water Tower** A nice bass held for a second against the water tower that was its undoing. Careful investigative work revealed that a colony of house martins was nesting just under the eaves of the tower. There were hundreds of nests, and each had a clutch of twittering babies. Tragically, every now and again, one of them would over-reach itself and drop helplessly into the water beneath. A closer look revealed that a good number of very sizeable bass had made the water tower their base, and anything life-like hitting the water close in from above was taken at once.

◀ **It's Mine!** What's happening here? I had just hooked into a small bass of around twelve to fourteen ounces on a small sub-surface lure. As I played the fish towards me, a much larger bass, a monster in fact, swirled up out of the depths, some five or so yards from my feet. At first, I thought that it was trying to eat the bass on the end of the line. However, when I got the photographs back, I realized that it was actually trying to pull my plug out of the small bass's mouth and take it for itself. If only it had managed to do so!

SPOONS AND SPINNERS

Spoons are simply pieces of shaped sheet metal, most commonly coloured silver or bronze. Many different types of spoon have been designed over the centuries, but all models can be cast and retrieved from the bank or from a boat, and can also be trolled behind the boat. When considering using a spoon, bear in mind its weight, colour and action, and how much flash it gives off, before making a choice.

A spinner has a blade that revolves quickly round a shaft. The angle of rotation, the speed of retrieve and the current all control how quickly the blade turns. The vibrations it produces and the flash of the blade attract pike and other predators.

Both spinners and spoons should be used with an anti-kink vane or attached to the main line by a freely rotating swivel to avoid line twist.

▲ **River Success** This angler is fishing a clear river, and clear water is generally preferred for spinner and spoon work. Both types of lure send out good, strong vibrations through the water, and predators can home in on these even in dull conditions, but sunlight has an advantage as it strikes the bright blades and sends out flashes of light through the water, and this really pulls the predators in.

Spinning for Grayling

Few people would think of spinning for grayling, but that's why I've included it here. Most fish species are more predatory than the average angler thinks and, at the right time of the year, virtually any type of fish will eat fish smaller than themselves. Bream can be predatory and so, amazingly, can roach, so it's not at all surprising that grayling will make a mouth at a small fish if they think the chances of success are high enough.

Of course, we're generally talking about larger grayling here. Fish of one and a half pounds and above will typically include fish in their diet on a regular basis, particularly in colder, more barren environments where insect life is limited. Arctic grayling come regularly to lures and very big flies, but even in more temperate Europe, spinning – if allowed – can pick up some surprisingly big fish.

Exploring the River You can cover a great deal of water by spinning, so if the grayling shoals are thin on the ground you still stand a good chance of making contact with them, especially if you are willing to wade. In winter they might be in big, deep slacks, but in summer and autumn try medium-paced water about five feet deep. Use the smallest spinner that you can cast successfully, and once you hit fish, move up in size to try and isolate the biggest fish.

Battle On Spinning for grayling calls for light tackle if you're going to get maximum enjoyment out of it. It's a good idea to cast the spinner slightly upriver and work it into the grayling's sight zone rather than out of it. This fish is being played on a modern spinning outfit – a light rod matched with a tiny reel, strong line and a box of small spinners.

Spinning for Murrel

Another odd one, you're thinking, but again I'm trying to make a point. Most people going fishing in India take extremely strong tackle and spend their entire days pursuing the mighty mahseer. Magnificent fish, admittedly, but there's an awful lot more going on in the Indian rivers that demands our attention. Top of the list, for me, is the sparkling murrel, which can provide huge entertainment. You find them in very shallow, virtually still water along the sides of the main river, close to weeds and reeds or behind rocks in shaded pools. Murrel are smash and grab predators that don't stray too far from cover to hit their prey, so a boat is a great help. You can reach the most inaccessible of places, and casting can be short and very precise indeed. A boat also has the added advantage of alerting the crocodiles, who make a discreet exit before your own appearance!

▸ **Taken in the Shallows** For a fish that looks very much like an eel, a murrel fights extremely well. From the first enormous crash that signals a take you know you're into something really special. They can grow to twenty pounds, but a ten-pounder will give you quite a scrap, leaping like a rainbow trout. Murrel tend to hunt by sight, so my guide gave this spinner a good polishing – and it worked!

▸ **A Happy Ghillie** Murrel are highly prized as a food fish, and it's almost impossible to convince the locals to let one go. Since learning that the female murrel actually guards her young for up to a year to prevent them being snaffled by predators, my compromise has been to fish for them but to slip the hook as soon as they come to the boat, and let them return to their offspring. It makes me unpopular back in camp but it eases my conscience.

Spinning for Char

Most people fly fish for Arctic char, but there's no harm in catching them on small spinners and light, balanced gear. In fact, in turbulent white water, where the glacial rivers really tumble to the sea, spinning has a big advantage. You can't wade, and the current almost immediately forms a belly in the fly line and whips the fly out of the taking zone. With spinning gear, you can cast further and keep the lure in the strike zone for longer. It's exciting and skilful stuff, and it demands great concentration. Cast a rod-handle's length too far or too short and you'll get nowhere. You have to be precise. You've also got to choose the right spinner – heavy enough to get through the roar of the water to the slightly easier paced stuff beneath, but not so heavy that it will plummet to the bottom and get snagged up.

◀ **A Thrilling Fight** These Arctic char straight from the freezing seas fight as hard as any other fish in the world pound for pound. They are surprisingly tender in the mouth and vulnerable to too much pressure, so I strongly advise using spinners with a single rather than a treble hook, and crushing the barb down. This makes unhooking much easier and the damage done to the mouth is kept to a minimum.

◀ **Many a Slip...** A good fish like this char might look beaten but it can easily turn and run and, on a short line, create a devastating break-off. Keep the rod high to absorb any unexpected lunges and slacken the clutch off a little so that it can give line easily. When you're wading in hard safe margins like this, it's a good idea to release each and every fish you hook in the water rather than taking it onto the bank, unless you absolutely need a trophy shot.

Spinning for Bass

Spinners are a useful addition to the bass fisherman's armoury, but they do get snagged in weed and it's hard to get them very close to features, where bass like to lie. The answer may be spinner baits, which are currently having huge success in the bass-fishing world. The elaborate spinner bait pulls bass out of the deepest cover with its combination of flash, action and colour, and its semi-snagless design makes it useful for fishing close to awkward features. It is, in essence, a combination of a spinner and a jig and, despite its amazing success rate, it resembles nothing that a bass would eat in the wild! Spinner baits also allow great freedom when it comes to choice of retrieve: a steady retrieve is possible, but you can also flip them across the surface or trawl them along the bottom.

▶ **Pinpoint Casting** At last, a decent bass has fallen for a spinner. It was hard work in clear water and blistering sunlight, but at least the shafts of sun really lit up the blade and made it dance. The bass were in a real following mood, often three or four fish patrolling the spinner out of their territory. It wasn't until Johnny began to work this particular spinner very, very close to the rocks indeed that we had any success at all.

▶ **Running Through the Box** I experimented with five different sizes of spinner and tried six different colours of blade before hitting this fish. Black proved to be the one, possibly because it gives a very definite silhouette on a hot day with bright sun. You can also try putting a tail on the spinner – wool, tinsel, a strip of bacon rind, a small plastic grub or even a couple of maggots.

Spinning for Perch

Small perch can be quite suicidal on any design of spinner you pull out of your box, but bigger fish become much more thoughtful. As when fishing for bass, it's a good idea to customize your spinner – for example, try putting red wool, hair, real or plastic worms, rubber skirts, thin strips of bacon or mackerel flesh on the trebles. Keep changing the spinner design: if a big perch has refused a spinner once, it's unlikely to take it on a second sighting. Once you get under the surface, the spinner becomes, to me at least, something of a blur – an indistinct vision of light patterns and colours. It does help, I personally believe, if a spinner has certain distinctive points of attraction to it: for example, a slash of red can imitate gills and I like to see a couple of big, black spots that look very much like eyes. Or do they? Perhaps they just give the fish a target to attack.

◀ **The Lily Bed** Wherever there is weed or any other feature in a pond, it's there that you'll find the perch stacked. Where you're unlikely to encounter them is in vast tracts of open water. If you're approaching a lily bed like this with a spinner, try and cast parallel to it so that you get as long a retrieve as possible. A spinner bait would probably be more effective in a heavily overgrown situation like this. You can even jig one in open holes amongst the pads. Remember to use especially strong line when fishing around lilies – let the fish get into the roots and you'll lose everything.

▲ **Striped Beauty** There's a bit of a story behind this very pretty fish. The setting was a very clear French river on a hot summer's day, so you could easily see the fish. I tried several different patterns of spinners before trying this particularly heavily-spotted one. What had proved a blank day immediately picked up. In all, I had about a dozen perch, but not the ones I was after – in the hole I was fishing were at least three fish of three pounds or more. One looked about four! Nothing I could do would tempt them, not even when I dug up some big, juicy lobs! A passing local suggested I catch one of the numerous lizards and let that trundle through the swim... I ask you!

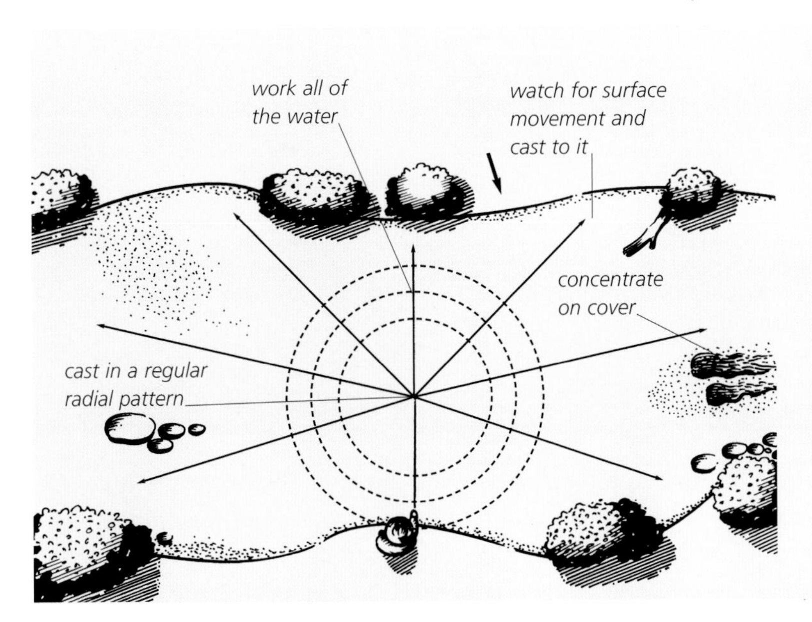

Radial Casting

Spinning for perch is often the best way to locate shoals – you can work a lot of the water and move on if no result is forthcoming. You often find perch near to snags, lying in ambush just like any other predator, but groups of fish will frequently patrol in open water. This is where radial casting comes in. Working your way 'round the clock' means that all the water is being systematically searched.

Spinning for Pike

Pike love spinners and have been caught on them for decades. Begin with small spinners that won't spook the fish, and then step up in size until you begin to hit fish. If the water's tinged with colour you'll probably end up using the biggest spinner you have in your box to flash out all the light available and to send a steady pulse through the water; but don't work your spinner too fast – the pike need time to home in on the bait and make a hit. When you're tackling pike, especially big ones, check the quality and size of the hooks on the spinner. It pays to fit them with strong, chemically sharpened hooks of the perfect size. I normally swear by barbless hooks, but for spinning I prefer a crushed down barb to make more strikes stick. Don't skimp on the length of your wire trace: I personally never settle for one of less than eighteen inches.

▲ **The Sunken Forest** This is the perfect territory to hunt pike out with any kind of lure. When fishing snags like this, it's absolutely irresponsible not to use the toughest of gear. You've got to hold the pike on the surface in such areas, because if you allow it to dive then it will soon be in the tree roots and lost, often taking your lure with it. Not good for the pocket, but especially bad for the fish.

Spoon Fishing for Pike

Spoon fishing is as simple a way of catching pike as any and it goes back centuries. My view is that spoon fishing is particularly effective for pike in spring and autumn when they are very active and willing to attack fast-moving lures. It works well, too, for perch, zander and even chub.

When it comes to spoon choice, start with size: four to six inches is just about perfect. A single hook is also preferable to a treble, because unhooking becomes so much easier, especially if you're not very experienced. As for colour, opt for silver in clear water, copper or brass if there's a tinge to the water and brightly-painted spoons when the water is really coloured. Also consider the weight of the spoon. Remember that getting the spoon to the correct depth is probably the real key to this style of fishing – even more important than the retrieve.

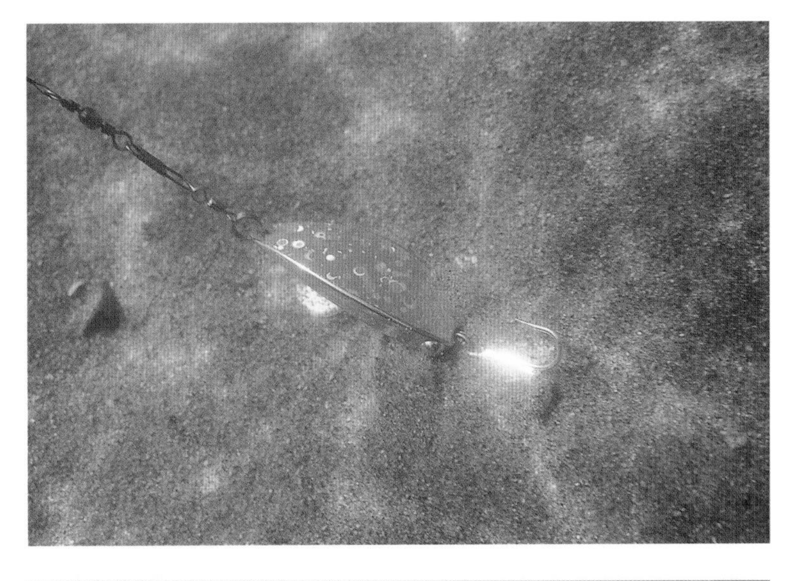

▸ **Sink and Draw** In deep water, when the pike are hugging the bottom you can use a heavy spoon like this rather as you would a dead bait, in the sink-and-draw style. Let the spoon go down and hit bottom, and then twitch it slowly back, lifting your rod tip so that it rises from time to time in the water. You'll often find that the pike hit it the moment it moves again or, very occasionally, will pick it from the bottom as it lies static.

▸ **Spinner Success** This is one of fifteen fish between four and twelve pounds taken in an afternoon's fishing. Don't make the mistake of thinking that spinners are only good for smaller pike. On British trout reservoirs in the past decade or so, they've accounted for fish of over forty pounds. And it's not true that only big baits will catch the biggest fish. Some very big pike have fallen to lures only a couple of inches long.

◀ **Short and Powerful** Don't go too long with your spoon rod – around nine feet is ideal. Choose a rod with a casting weight of twenty to sixty grams. Marry this with a fixed-spool reel and, providing the water isn't too snaggy, braid. Fifty-pound breaking strain is not over the top. If you are going to use a single-hook spoon, which I personally recommend, make sure the hook is the strongest you can buy.

◀ **Irish Delight** This is my great friend, Richie Johnson, one of the great Irish pikers and a man who has consistently sworn by the magic of spoon fishing. Richie sets a perfect example, always experimenting with different spoon sizes, shapes, colours and weights. He's also a master at varying the rate of retrieve. The clarity of many Irish waters makes spoon fishing an ideal method.

◀ **Backwaters** It's a good idea to explore little channels and backwaters like this with a weedless spoon, one with a wire guard over the hook to stop it picking up weed and other rubbish. If the water is very shallow, then you'll have to skim the spoon just under the surface. If the bottom isn't too snaggy, it often pays, however, to let it flutter down and just settle for a few seconds before recommencing the retrieve.

▶ **Spring Delight** I caught this fish in very late March when the water was really beginning to warm up quickly. It's now that the pike are particularly active and willing to hit a lure that's moving quite close to the surface at a reasonable speed. With fish of this size you can choose quite a large spoon, say about six inches. If you're working it high in the water, don't go for one with heavy, thick metal. By contrast, when the pike are down deep, you've got to get the spoon down there. Cast a heavy spoon out, and when it hits the water leave the bale arm open until line has stopped leaving the spool and it's hit bottom. This is risky in very snaggy water, so use braid of no less than fifty-pound breaking strain. Remember, the snaggiest areas produce the biggest fish.

▲ **Trolling** Trolled spoons are very effective on large waters. To get any depth, you'll need a downrigger or, more simply, perhaps a two-ounce lead on the line. If water clarity isn't too good, choose a big spoon that rotates as much as possible to send out really strong vibrations. Lightweight spoons can be effective when the water is very clear and warm and the depths aren't too great. As you can see here, multiplier reels are used, and they are particularly good for trolling.

Trolling Lures

The depth at which your lure is working is critical. You can make sure lures are worked high in the water by retrieving them under a small float. You can bounce the lure along the bottom by taking it down with a lead attached to a weak link, but most lake beds are too rocky for this approach. Think carefully about your trolling speed, too. Experiment until you find a speed that provokes most of the takes. Also vary your boat's course, as many predators strike as the lure changes direction in the water.

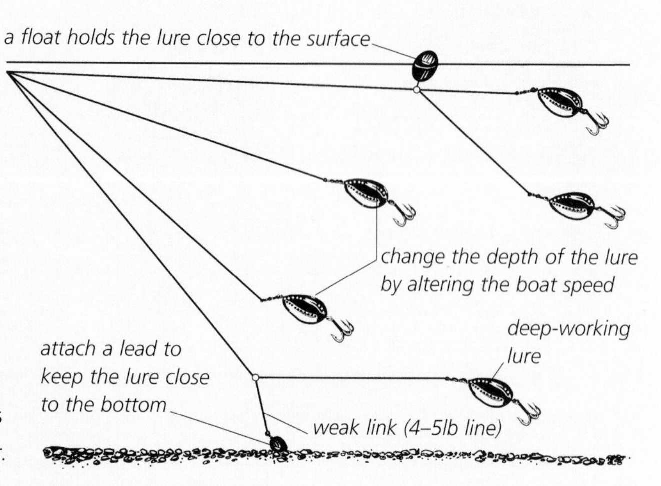

◀ **Baltic Offerings** This is a beautiful fish taken from the Baltic Sea – note its wonderful silver colour and marvellous markings. The whole Baltic coastline is ideal for spoon fishing. In its shallow, bright, clear water you can use a silver spoon with fairly thin metal so that it doesn't catch continually on the bottom. Retrieve it quickly, sometimes skipping it on the surface. If you want to go further out, onto the sea itself, it's quite possible to move to a bigger, thicker, heavier spoon that gets down deeper. Takes when trolling are often really big hits, so do be prepared. Either hold the rod or make sure it's very securely in a good, firm rod rest. It's also a good idea to tie the handle of the rod with a piece of rope attached to the boat seat. It never pays to take risks.

PLUGS

Plugs are age-old – usually simple creations fashioned out of wood or hard plastic to mimic a small prey fish. A plug has an in-built swimming action, but it's up to the angler to impart life to it. Top-water plugs, which are used primarily in warmer weather, crash and vibrate on the surface, attracting predators through both sight and sound. Shallow divers work down to about six feet or so. Many are also buoyant, so they begin the retrieve on the surface itself. Next, we have the deep divers, plugs that can go down to forty feet or more. These are the tools of the big, clear lakes, particularly in North America, where pike or lake trout are being sought. Mention should also be made of jerk baits, the big beasts of the lure jungle, which have built up a huge reputation for large fish. Most jerk baits float and to work well depend on the angler ripping them down from the surface – hard work, but worth the effort.

▲ **All Shapes and Sizes** Not all plugs are large creations of wood, metal or plastic. Small plugs, such as the Crystal River Hopper, can be used on fly tackle to catch pike, perch, chub and bass.

The Behaviour of Plugs

To get the best out of plug fishing, you need to know just how a plug behaves under the water. Seek out some very clear, shallow water, which has a good hard bottom where you can wade, and study the action of your plug. How fast does the plug sink? If it's a buoyant plug, how quickly does it rise back towards the surface? How does a plug respond to a jerk-type retrieve? Try casting the plug as far as you can – does it tangle in flight? Do you need to feather the spool to prevent this? Look carefully at the hooks. Are they sharp enough. Are they strong enough for the fishing that you have in mind? If not, substitute them with larger, heavier hooks but, once again, test them in shallow, clear water to make sure that the action isn't compromised. The following shots show my own experiments.

◀ **On the Dive** When a plug dives steeply, the tail treble collapses onto the body and, sometimes, this prevents a secure hook hold, resulting in a missed take. Here, I'm looking into ways of making sure that the tail treble remains out rigid. This is one of my favourite lures – the Shad Rap – which has often rescued the day when everything else has failed.

◀ **A Slow Rise** You'd be surprised just how many predators grab a plug when it is not actually being retrieved by you, but is simply rising or falling in the water. Even if you're not actually retrieving, it's vitally important to watch your line very carefully for any suspicious signs of tightening or slackening. Notice how this plug hangs like a typical prey fish.

▶ **The Retrieve** The shape, size and angle of the diving blade – the lip of the plug – determine how a plug dives and works through the water. Look carefully at how each of the plugs you test works and try a number of retrieve techniques. This should give you some indication of what method makes the lure look enticing. Personally, I like to retrieve any type of lure slowly – just bring it back quickly enough to get the action on the move.

▶ **Staying Deep** Sometimes it pays to get a plug down to the very bottom, especially in cold weather when predators are fairly comatose. Going down deep and retrieving slowly can be a real winner. Pike respond to low-frequency vibrations, so the speed at which you retrieve that lure could really be the most important factor of all.

How a Pike Locates a Lure

A pike has sharp eyesight, especially in decent light and clear water when it can probably see its prey up to twenty yards away, but in low light or muddy water it resorts to vibration and smell for prey location. A moving lure – especially one that rattles – attracts predators by the vibrations that it sends out through the water. These are picked up by sensitive detectors along the fish's lateral line.

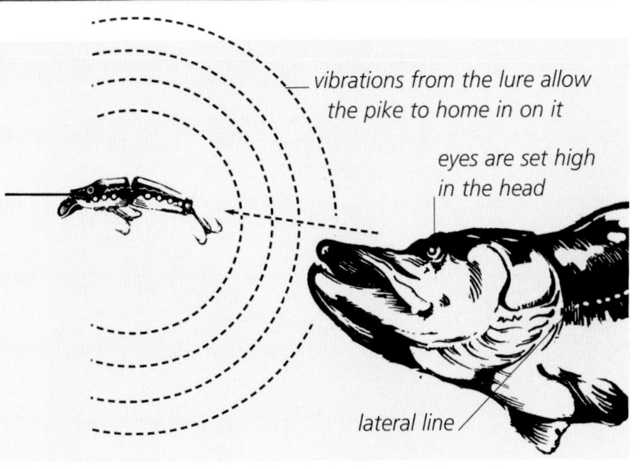

Plugging the World

There's barely a country in the world that doesn't have some species that respond to plugs voraciously. In the USA, you have northern pike, muskies, bass, walleye and perch, as well as numerous members of the salmonid family. In Europe, there's pike, zander, asp, chub, perch, ferox trout and, from time to time, catfish. In Africa, you have Nile perch and tiger fish. In Australia, a barramundi likes nothing more than a big, juicy plug. Finally, in Latin America, where just about everything eats everything else, a plug that isn't built like a tank is mincemeat in seconds. If you are lucky enough to travel, watch the local experts at work. You'd be amazed how each community has built up its own skills. In Siberia, for example, I've seen the crudest gear imaginable put to successful use, shaming my own efforts with gear a hundred times more sophisticated.

◀ **Fun Fishing** Plugging is especially good in warm, clear water, so it's a method that's applicable almost worldwide. Drum fish, bonito, snapper, barramundi, barracuda, jack and tarpon are all warm water fish with a liking for plugs. Sally enjoys fishing for smaller bass and barramundi that fight well on sensible gear in relatively shallow water.

◀ **Barbel on a Plug!** More fish are predatory than you might think. I took this shot of a giant comizo barbel beside a central Spanish river, and it had been taken on a plug. These fish reach forty pounds and look very much like *barbus barbus*, the common barbel of Europe. However, these fish don't get as large as this without turning to a predatorial diet now and again.

Trolling with Plugs

In its simplest form, trolling is simply pulling spoons or plugs through the water at any given depth behind a moving boat. It sounds easy in theory, but in practice there's a huge amount to the method. For a start, you need to be able to master a boat, sometimes in rough conditions. You've also got to assemble the right gear and know exactly the depth at which your lures are working. Then, you've got to think how best to make them work and at what speed. Next, you have to decide where best to fish in a water that may be many miles in length and hundreds of feet in depth. After all that, when you get a take, you need to control the boat and play what is often a big fish without tangle or hazard.

▸ **A Fine Lake Trout** Trolling is the best way to catch a big water trout, such as this lake trout. These fish live in great, deep, featureless lakes and you need to cover as much water as possible to find them. The action of your plug will be defined by the speed at which it is trolled. So, if you're using a new lure, troll just under the water surface, close to the boat, for a few minutes. Watch the lure to see how best to set the engine throttle for peak performance.

▸ **Tools of the Trade** Once you're happy that the plug is working well, make a mental note of how the rod tip is behaving. The rod tip usually starts to bounce and vibrate when the best trolling speed of the lure is reached. Look here at the tools of the troller's trade – oars, engine, echo sounder, downrigger and, although you can't see it, an unhooking mat on the floor of the boat.

▲ **Swedish Beast** Not all trolling has to be deep. Here, Johnny holds a magnificent Swedish pike to the camera. It was taken in a bay no more than a yard deep, and on a very buoyant, tiny plug. It was being trolled just a couple of rod lengths behind the boat and we could see the pike come to the plug, follow it, inspect it and suddenly turn its head and suck it in. As it was hooked in such shallow water, it could only run far, not deep, and at times it forced the boat to follow.

▲ **Bass Techniques** There is a tendency to think of fishing for bass – even spectacular ones such as this peacock bass – as being up close, all tight and intimate, but even with these fabulous fish there are times when it pays to get distance between the boat and the predator. Trolling can do this, and is also an excellent way to locate fish in any large water. You can troll a couple of baits until you begin to get hits and then anchor up and fish the water with a variety of methods.

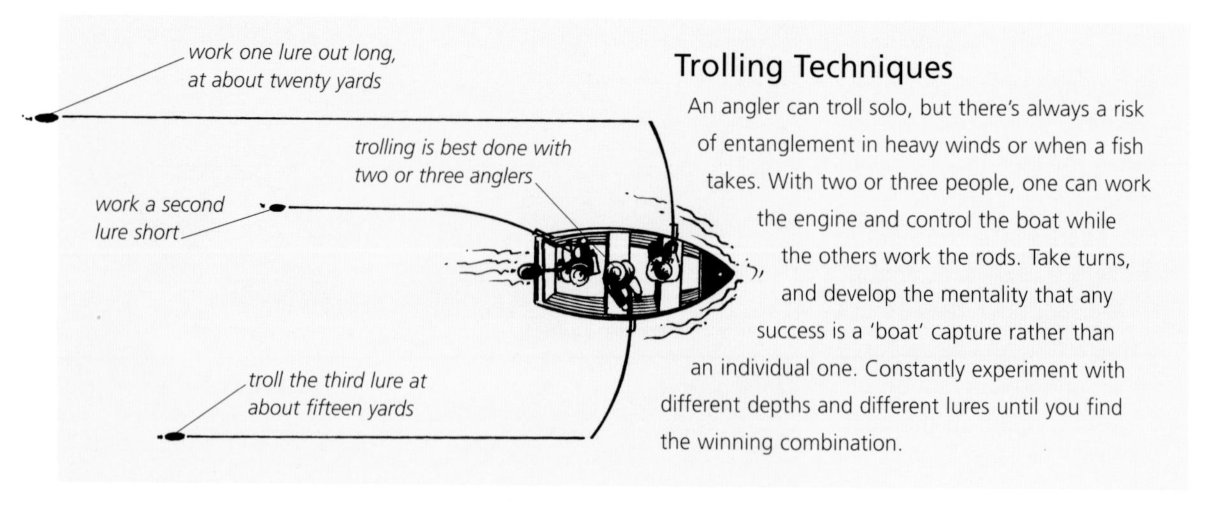

Trolling Techniques

An angler can troll solo, but there's always a risk of entanglement in heavy winds or when a fish takes. With two or three people, one can work the engine and control the boat while the others work the rods. Take turns, and develop the mentality that any success is a 'boat' capture rather than an individual one. Constantly experiment with different depths and different lures until you find the winning combination.

▲ **Monsters of Africa** Here you see two of my most respected fishing colleagues, Jim and Linda, with the results of an extraordinary day's fishing. Nile perch are the kings of the African continent and can only really be caught by trolling. Very big lures, strong rods and well-filled reels are the order of the day. As for killing the fish… well, the life of a sporting fish is very important, but it can't take precedence over the needs of a village whose children are malnourished.

▲ **Windermere, England** In the right hands, trolling can produce some tremendous bonuses. For many years, Lake Windermere – England's largest lake – was considered average for both pike and ferox trout. Then, the experts began to fish the water with modern methods, new plug designs and an open mind. The results over the last few years have been extraordinary – Windermere has now been shown to hold larger pike and trout than was ever thought possible.

The Downrigger

A downrigger allows you to troll a lure very deep indeed, way past its normal working depth. Also, you can play the fish freely, for when it takes, the reel line is snapped away from the downrigger's cable. Operate the downrigger from the stern of the boat, and lower the rig down with the winch provided. A word of caution: don't use a downrigger if you're fishing solo. If the trolling weight snags and you're in a heavy wind a small boat can be put at severe risk. The downrigger is particularly useful on glacial waters where depths frequently exceed two or, even, three hundred feet.

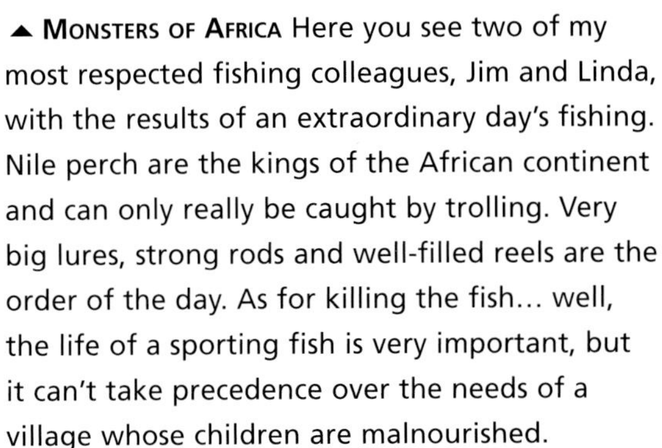

Choice of Plugs

Many experts, in the bass world particularly, talk about finding the right match or 'pattern'. By this, they mean clicking with the right style of fishing at a particular time. For example, you wouldn't choose a surface-fishing plug in the middle of winter when the water is close to freezing and the pike are down deep. Equally, if the pike are lying in shallow, sun-warmed bays, you wouldn't choose a great big, heavy trolling spoon or a plug that works best at forty feet! At its basic level, this is simply common sense, but the more experienced you become the more you'll tweak the options. Certainly, when you're under water, you begin to see just how wrong some lures look in certain conditions – they just stick out like a sore thumb... although, it must be said, sometimes that's exactly what they should do!

◀ **Clouded Water** This shot of an orange Shad Rap was taken in water with very poor visibility. What is interesting, though, is the fact that the auto-focus camera could zoom in on this plug, even at some distance, but could not do so with a plug of any other colour. This seems to suggest that, in murky water at least, an orange lure stands more chance of being picked out than a green or brown one.

◀ **Plugging in Spain** This is the small plug on which the large comizo barbel was caught in a central Spanish river (see page 78). Its action is designed to get right down to the bed quickly and bounce among the rocks – and it certainly did the trick.

▶ **Large Plugs** When the river was unexpectedly coloured, we found that all the predators would hit much bigger lures than normal. In fact, one of my colleagues began to catch fish on this huge mid-European creation that was at least eleven inches long. It was almost impossible to cast and landed like a tree trunk! Still, it did the trick.

▼ **Hitting Rock** In clear water, it can be a good idea to let your plug hit bottom once or twice. On a rock bottom this will send out vibrations, and on a muddy riverbed it will send up a cloud of silt that can give the impression of an escaping crayfish. In very clear water, sometimes the unexpected works well. If you see a predator homing in, try slackening off to let the lure rise towards the surface or, if it's a spoon, sink towards the bottom. Don't be afraid to try the unusual to trigger a take.

Plugging for Taiman

I make no apology for bringing up Mongolian taiman again. To put it simply, if you can get taiman plugging right, then you can succeed anywhere with any fish. The water in Mongolian rivers is ice cold, crystal clear and frequently pouring through like an express train – three aspects that make everything you do critical. The taiman itself is supremely wild and suspicious, and my underwater experiences suggest they have possibly the best eyesight of any predator. You certainly need to try every trick in the lure angler's book to be consistently successful. One tip for here, and anywhere else where you can't use a boat and where long casting is essential, is to feather your line against the spool on the cast so that the plug doesn't tangle with the leader. To do this, simply control the rate of line coming off the reel with your index or middle finger. Some casting distance will be lost by feathering, but you can guarantee a good tangle-free retrieve every time.

◀ **Jerk Baits** This shot was taken a few years ago, before I really got the hang of true jerk-bait fishing. You need a short, stiff rod that can really hammer out a long cast, and a multiplier reel is much better than a fixed-spool for this. After casting, a quick pull will get the bait moving. As you feel it slow down, another pull keeps it moving through the water. Make sure your line-retrieval rate is smooth and consistent. It will also help if you fill the spool of your reel to maximum capacity. Don't go light for this sort of fishing – fifty-pound braid or upwards is about right. If you're really throwing lures out, you could even consider eighty- or 100-pound braid. You'll also need a really solid wire trace to prevent tangling – a 150-pound breaking strain wire will suffice.

▸ **Shallow Water** Taiman often come into very shallow water to hunt their prey – basically trout and grayling – and in this they are like any other predator. Look carefully for the signs of feeding fish, whatever your quarry. The choice now is between a top lure or a sub-surface one. Sub-surface lures are probably easier to manipulate and more strikes stick with them, but for a real heart-in-the-mouth experience you can't beat the sight of a bow wave looming up behind a chugging, popping, top-water crawler!

▸ **Imitating Nature** This fascinating creation, designed to look exactly like a lenok trout, was made by a master plug expert in the Czech Republic. It possesses an excellent action in the water, as does his imitation of a baby taiman – another preferred food item of this very big fish.

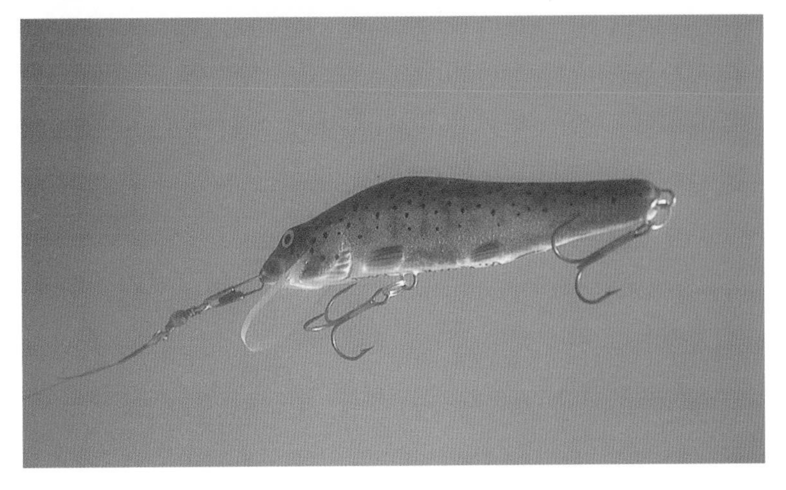

CONSERVATION

Predators may look tough and toothy, but they're as vulnerable as any other fish. In many waters, we, the anglers, are their primary predators once they have grown; we are the one species capable of harming or even killing them. It's up to us to try to make our meetings with them as stress-free as possible. Indeed, if you follow a well-defined code of practice, it's possible to go through a lifetime of catching fish without causing any casualties whatsoever. There are basic considerations: firstly, realize that fish do take on stress during a battle; accept that the shorter the time they are out of the water, the better; keep calm at all times, both during the fight and when the fish is on the bank; and get to work unhooking your predator with confidence, with knowledge and with the right tools at your disposal.

▲ **Mongolian Treasure** John Chester supports a huge Mongolian taiman half in and half out of the water. A pose like this is very kind to the fish: stress is minimized and the gut of the fish remains supported.

The Treatment of Wild Fish

Wild fish? Surely all fish are wild, I hear you say. Well, true, but, in my eyes, some fish are wilder than others! I believe that fish who have rarely, or even never, encountered humans react to them in a much more fundamental fashion if and when our paths cross, and an angler can cause considerable stress in a virgin river.

Many anglers are travelling to remote and unfished places nowadays; it's a simple fact of piscatorial life, and I'd like to offer some guidelines to those who do. Firstly, wild fish are much more easily caught than those with an element of education about them. Please, therefore, show restraint, and realize that it's not always necessary to catch a bagful. Secondly, a lot of untouched waters are in extreme environments – either very hot or very cold. Extreme temperatures only increase the problems of stress for the fish.

If we are privileged enough to find ourselves a practically virgin stream, surely it's our duty, as guardians of the environment, to make sure that that stream is as pure when we leave as when we arrived – we should never sully the wilderness.

▶ **To Hand** Always remember that no fish, however wild, relishes being taken from the water, any more than we enjoy being pulled into it. In many situations, especially if the margins are shallow and safe and you are wearing thigh boots or chest waders, it is quite possible to unhook a fish without lifting it bodily from its environment. Never use trebles larger than you need. Use fine wire if you can. Try using singles, and try going barbless. Always ensure that your hands are wet before touching a fish. Then, simply put pliers to the hook, twist, and the fish should swim free. Support it in the shallows until it is strong enough to swim away with no danger of it turning over in the current.

◀ **Careful Release** When returning any predator, hold it against a gentle current, if there is one, and simply wait for the fish to make its own decision when to leave. What you see here is fine, but never, ever hold a fish by the tail out of the water – unless you're going to kill the fish instantly afterwards – as you will pull the fish's whole bone structure out of joint and condemn it to a lingering death.

◀ **Pride and Joy** I really like this photograph of my great friend Christopher West looking admiringly at a beautiful trout that has a mouth big enough to swallow a whale! He has played the fish out and is kneeling in the water preparing to release it. The barbs on the hook have been flattened, which will make release easier. Notice, too, that he's not using a net – there's always a chance that the fish will spin in a net and that the front trebles will become attached to a piece of flesh or even an eye. Chris is about to take his forceps from the pocket of his chest waders and simply flick the treble clear. The fish has not been taken out of the water and, with sensitive treatment like this, it's likely to be feeding again before the end of the day.

Preserving Pike

Throughout the history of pike fishing, in virtually every water that has been fished, man has proved to be the threat to the fish stocks. The damage used to be wilful: in the relatively recent past, anglers throughout the northern hemisphere would demand their trophy – a dead fish in its entirety or just the head to be sent to the taxidermist to be stuffed. Such practices are, thankfully, largely in the past, but there are still major errors when it comes to handling pike. Some of this is through ignorance: there's simply not enough advice given on how to handle a pike on the bank. Some of the problems come through fear. After all, that mouth full of sharp, inwardly-pointing teeth does look a pretty formidable proposition. It needn't be if you're calm, cool and know what you're doing.

▲ **Playing a Fish** Make sure that your gear is man enough for the job, or you run the risk of a break-off and leaving the fish with a hook lodged in its mouth. Play a fish steadily and with confidence, and never prolong a battle to enjoy more sport. Similarly, don't bully a fish so that it comes to the bank still lively and in a mood to thrash about. Remember, too, that fish often fight more furiously in summer than in winter, so be prepared.

▼ **Dead-Bait Striking** This is a worrying photograph. The pike is coming to the net, but neither the dead bait nor the hooks are in sight. This is bound to mean a deep-hooked fish. The old rule on dead-bait striking was to wait for the second run, but the humane advice is to strike as soon as a run develops. Okay, some pike will be missed, but they'll usually be small fish, and if you use a relatively small dead bait you'll hook most decent pike.

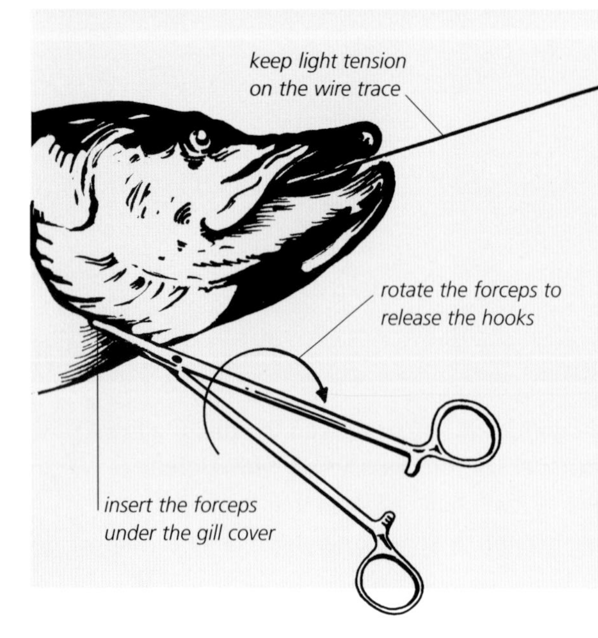

Unhooking Down Deep

There are times when a pike will take either a lure or a dead bait down deep and then you've got to go in through the gills. Keep a light tension on the wire trace and use long-nosed forceps for this job. Be very careful not to injure the gills themselves and if the hooks are barbless you stand a good chance of being able to slip them out without too much danger. A pair of strong wire cutters can be useful to cut a hook that is really firmly lodged in. Always have a first aid kit with you, especially if you hand-land your fish. You can always tell a successful pike angler at any meeting by the number of plasters he'll have on his fingers!

▲ **When to Use a Net** I tend to feel that nets are best avoided if possible and that hand-landing a fish is safer, but for the times when you need it, buy the largest net you can find. Use a net until you are confident of lifting out a large predator by hand or if you are fishing from a steep bank. Never put your net into the water until the fish is tired and absolutely ready. A flying treble can easily get caught in the mesh if it's held beneath the water's surface when the fish is not yet tired.

▶ **On the Bank** If you need a trophy shot, like this one of a rare and exotic Amur pike, then make sure that you've got all the necessary equipment. You certainly should have an unhooking mat and a weighing sling if you want to record the fish accurately. Forceps, long-nosed pliers and wire cutters should all be ready to hand and, if you're on your own, make sure your camera is already on its tripod, set up, focused and ready to go.

◀ **A Stressful Experience** Some time ago, I saw a couple of youngsters catch this pike of about five pounds, unhook it not particularly well and keep it out of the water for an overly-long time. In fact, I talked to them about it. Eventually, the fish was released and, some five or ten minutes later I came across it in three feet of water. As you can see, the stress has drained the head of blood and the pale, blotchy markings are typical of a pike that has suffered trauma.

▼ **Not Feeding, but Hiding** And this is the same traumatized pike shortly afterwards, actually burrowing into the silt, probably as a defence mechanism. However, coincidentally, pike often act like this when they are hunting eels and small flatfish in the mud. Pike are active hunters and will earn their living in many different ways. If you see a cloud form on the surface of the water, with bubbles coming up, it may not be a tench, carp or bream. It's worth putting a deep-working plug or lure through the area.

The Need for Research

It's not just what we fishermen on the bank do that helps fish and fisheries. Proper scientific research is also required if the predators that we love are going to be conserved and looked after in a decent fashion. For many years, trout and salmon have cornered the market in research terms because of their financial clout, but as sport fishing becomes more important, hopefully it will attract more research resources. Believe me, research saves lives. You don't have to go far back – if at all in certain areas – to find a time when the owners of trout fisheries used to kill all pike for what they believed was the good of their stocks. When proper scientific research kicked in it showed that if big pike were killed, then jack pike, the real critters in any fishery, proliferated. It was the big pike that actually kept the small pike under control. Enlightened trout fishery owners now return the bigger pike knowing full well that without them their fisheries will be far less viable. Good news for the trout, for the pike and for those who love to fish for them.

▲ **Meet Dennis** Some years ago Christopher and I were paid – yes paid – to catch and electronically tag ferox trout. We named the fish we caught after Scottish heroes, and this is Dennis Law, pictured moments before release. I'd always believed that ferox, like pike, tended to hole up and wait for char shoals to come to them. The tagging of Dennis and other ferox showed that in actual fact ferox spend a great deal, if not all, of their lives on the drift, following the deep, underwater currents. This finding taught me to troll as much of the loch as I could to maximize my chances of an encounter.

Author's Acknowledgements

My greatest thanks for encouragement, inspiration, generosity and friendship go to Johnny Jensen and Martin Hayward Smith; both are expert photographers who have collaborated with me so closely on these works – I cannot possibly overstate their contribution.

Thank you also to Kevin Cullimore for showing me the way, back in the 1990s. Thank you to the late and dearly missed Mike Smith at Bure Valley Fisheries, Mike Taylor at the Red Lion in Bredwardine, Bill Makins at Pensthorpe and Paul Seaman for all your help with locations.

Thank you in Spain to Peter, Rafa, Ignatio and José… marvellous men and anglers all.

Thank you to all the following for your help, either in fishing situations or for your copious and wise advice: Alan Felstead, Leo Grosze Nipper, Sue and Chris Harris, Reuben Hook, Phil Humm, Simon MacMillan, Robert Malone, Rob Olsen, Christopher West and Jo Whorisky.

Thank you to Steve at Ocean Optronics, and to Fergus Granville in North Uist.

Thank you to all at Design Revolution, and special thanks to Carol, who has had to contend with a mass of woolly-minded thoughts from yours truly.